MW01173056

Diabetic Air Fryer Cookbook

365 Days Quick and Delicious Recipes with Inexpensive Ingredients to Lower Your Blood Sugar for Type 2 Diabetes and Prediabetes | 28 Days Healthy Meal Plan

By

Nathan Terrell

© Copyright 2022 by Nathan Terrell - All rights reserved.

This document is geared towards providing exact and reliable information regarding the topic and issue covered. The publication is sold with the idea that the publisher is not required to render accounting, officially permitted, or otherwise, qualified services. If advice is necessary, legal, or professional, a practiced individual in the profession should be ordered.

- From a Declaration of Principles which was accepted and approved equally by a Committee of the American Bar Association and a Committee of Publishers and Associations.

In no way is it legal to reproduce, duplicate, or transmit any part of this document in either electronic means or in printed format. Recording of this publication is strictly prohibited and any storage of this document is not allowed unless with written permission from the publisher. All rights reserved.

The information provided herein is stated to be truthful and consistent, in that any liability, in terms of inattention or otherwise, by any usage or abuse of any policies, processes, or directions contained within is the solitary and utter responsibility of the recipient reader. Under no circumstances will any legal responsibility or blame be held against the publisher for any reparation, damages, or monetary loss due to the information herein, either directly or indirectly.

Respective authors own all copyrights not held by the publisher.

The information herein is offered for informational purposes solely and is universal as so. The presentation of the information is without contract or any type of guarantee assurance.

The trademarks that are used are without any consent, and the publication of the trademark is without permission or backing by the trademark owner. All trademarks and brands within this book are for clarifying purposes only and are the owned by the owners themselves, not affiliated with this document.

Table of Contents

Introduction

Public health professionals would declare it a crisis if diabetes type 2 were a contagious illness that spread from person to person. Due to the rising rates of pediatric obesity, this challenging condition is now affecting an increasing number of adults as well as more and more children, particularly those belonging to certain ethnic groups. The great news is that type 2 diabetes and prediabetes may both be substantially avoided. Making lifestyle adjustments may prevent almost nine out of ten instances. The risk of acquiring heart disease and various malignancies may be decreased by making the same modifications. Five words sum up the secret to prevention, i.e. Stay active and Stay lean. If you have been diagnosed with diabetes already, advice for avoiding or reducing your risk of acquiring type 2 diabetes is also appropriate. Blood glucose regulation is enhanced by maintaining healthy body weight, eating a balanced & carbohydrate-controlled diet, and exercising often.

A healthy lifestyle for someone with diabetes entails both activity and proper diet. A balanced diet & frequent exercise can help you keep your blood glucose, commonly referred to as the sugar, within the target range, among other benefits. You should balance what you eat and drink with exercise and diabetes medicines, if you consume any, in order to regulate your blood glucose. Initially, it could seem challenging to become more active and change your drinking and eating routines. It can be easier for you to start small and ask the assistance of your family, friends, and medical professionals.

Diabetics can consume air-fried meals as part of a balanced diet. However, it's advised to restrict how often you consume such kinds of dishes each day, just as with any item that is fried in oil (little or big). Although it isn't a miraculous treatment for diabetes, it may assist those with the disease in choosing healthier alternatives to deep-fried meals. The amount of fat you consume and the number of saturated fats you consume may both be decreased using an air fryer. You may enjoy your favorite dishes in an air fryer without worrying about consuming too many calories. These little tools provide a healthier dinner with less fat and sugar by cooking food fast and uniformly. The most crucial aspect of utilizing an air fryer to prepare healthy meals is to cook them at the prescribed temperature. Not just proteins but a variety of veggies may be cooked in air fryers. They reduce the amount of oil used and the number of calories in deep-fried meals. Air fryers are beneficial for diabetes. Additionally, they let individuals eat "fried" meals without worrying about gaining weight or becoming ill from too much oil, which is particularly beneficial if you have diabetes. Food may be made more nutritious and with fewer carbs by using air fryers. Contrarily, air frying and deep frying are dangerous cooking techniques that increase the production of acrylamide, which, when ingested in excess, may lead to cancer & other health issues.

Chapter 1: Understanding Diabetes Type 2 & Benefits of an Air Fryer for Diabetics

Type 2 diabetes may be challenging to control if you are overweight or obese. Additionally, it raises the risk of high blood pressure and cholesterol, both of which are precursors to cardiovascular disease, the main killer of diabetes patients. You can better control your diabetes by leading a healthy lifestyle. Your vital health indicators, such as weight, blood pressure, blood sugar, and blood cholesterol, may also improve. Eating well and increasing your physical activity are two strategies for weight management.

It might be challenging to avoid junk food and fried foods while eating a balanced diet. When you've diabetes, fried meals are often not allowed, or they are not advised at least. However, fried meals cooked in air fryers are more suitable for a diabetic diet. You should be aware of the fact that air frying is healthier than conventional frying since it consumes fewer calories and less fat than traditional frying in oil. As a result, air-fried meals are preferable if you have diabetes and want to shed or maintain your weight, particularly if you're diabetic.

1.1 Understanding Diabetes

Diabetes occur when cells of your body are not able to absorb glucose (sugar) & utilize it as fuel. As a consequence, your bloodstream begins to accumulate additional sugar. Diabetes that is not properly managed may have catastrophic effects

and harm a number of bodily organs and tissues, including the heart, kidneys, eyes, and nerves. In the United States, 34.2 million individuals of all ages, or nearly 1 in 10, have diabetes. One in five persons (approximately 7.3 million) over the age of 18 does not know they've diabetes (just below 3 percent of all adults). As individuals become older, more people are getting diabetes diagnoses. One in four persons (more than 26%) who are 65 years of age or older has diabetes.

Why it occurs:

Your body breaks the food you consume into different nutritional sources as part of the digesting process. Your body converts carbs (such as bread, rice, and pasta) you consume into

sugar (glucose). When sugar is in circulation, it requires assistance—a "key"—to enter your body's cells, which make up the body's organs and tissues and are where it will be utilized. Insulin serves as this support or "key." The pancreas, an organ situated beneath the stomach, is the gland that produces the hormone insulin. Insulin is released into your bloodstream by your pancreas. The "door" in the cell wall is unlocked by insulin, allowing glucose to enter the cells of your body. The "fuel" or energy that tissues & organs need to operate effectively is provided by glucose.

Having diabetes:

- Insufficient or no insulin is produced by your pancreas.

Or

- Insulin is produced by your pancreas, but your body's cells do not react to it and cannot utilize it as they should. Your glucose level in the blood will increase if glucose cannot enter your body's cells and instead remains in circulation.

Symptoms:

Diabetes symptoms include:

- Enhanced thirst
- Weak and exhausted.
- Distorted vision
- Tingling or numbness in the feet or hands.
- Slow-healing wounds or sores.
- Unexpected weight loss
- A lot of urine.
- Frequent infections without a known cause.
- Dry mouth.

Additional signs:

- Frequently occurring urinary tract or yeast infections in women, as well as dry, itchy skin.
- Erectile dysfunction diminished muscle strength and decreased sex desire in males.

Types:

Diabetes Types include:

Type 1 (insulin-dependent) Diabetes: It's an autoimmune condition in which the body assaults itself. In this situation, your pancreas' insulin-making cells are killed. Type 1 (insulin-dependent) diabetes have its effects on up to ten percent of those who have the disease. Typically, children & young adults get the diagnosis (but anyone can get it). Diabetes was more often recognized as "juvenile" diabetes. Those who have this diabetes should take insulin daily. It is also called insulin-dependent form of diabetes for this reason.

Type 2 (adult-onset) diabetes: In this kind, either your body doesn't produce sufficient insulin, or your cells don't react to it properly. The most typical kind of diabetes is this one. This diabetes have its effect on up to ninety five percent of persons with the disease. People in their middle years and older tend to develop it. Insulin-resistant diabetes and adults-onset diabetes are two more names for Type 2.

Pre-diabetes: This condition is a precursor to diabetes Type 2. Your glucose levels in the blood are above average but not that high to get a diabetes Type 2 diagnosis.

Gestational diabetes: This kind appears in certain pregnant women. After pregnancy, the gestational diabetes often disappears. However, if you've gestational diabetes, you are more prone to eventually acquire diabetes Type 2.

It may occur in less prevalent forms like:

Monogenic diabetic syndromes: Up to 4% of all instances of diabetes are caused by these uncommon hereditary variants of the disease. Examples include young-onset diabetes with maturity and neonatal diabetes.

Diabetes associated with cystic fibrosis: This is a kind of diabetes that only affects those who have this condition.

Diabetes brought on by drugs or chemicals: Symptoms of this kind include organ transplantation, HIV/AIDS therapy, and usage of glucocorticoids.

Diabetes insipidus: Your kidneys create a lot of pee when you have diabetes insipidus, a unique, unusual illness.

Complications:

Your body's tissues & organs may sustain severe harm if your glucose level in blood is increased for a long length of time. Over the course of time, certain issues may pose a danger to life. One's complications are:

- Cardiovascular conditions such as atherosclerosis, hypertension, heart attack, high cholesterol, and chest discomfort (narrowing of arteries).

- Numbness and tingling brought on by neuropathy (nerve injury) that begins at the toes or fingers and progresses.

- Nephropathy, or damage to the kidneys, may cause renal failure and the requirement for dialysis or a kidney transplant.

- Blindness-results in eye degeneration known as retinopathy, cataracts, and glaucoma.

- The foot injury includes bad blood flow, nerve damage, and slow wound and pain healing.

- Infected skin.

- Erection problems.

- Loss of hearing.

- Depression.

- Dementia.

- Dental issues.

1.2 Type 2 Diabetes - Brief Explanation

A serious illness known as type 2 diabetes occurs when your pancreas is unable to produce enough insulin or when the insulin it does produce cannot function correctly. This indicates that your blood sugar (glucose) levels are increasing. In the UK, type 2 diabetes affects around 90% of those who have it. It is a severe ailment that may last a lifetime. If type 2 diabetes is left untreated, excessive blood sugar levels may gravely harm several body organs, such as your feet, heart, and eyes. These are referred to as diabetic complications. You may live well with diabetes type 2 and lower your chance of acquiring it, however, with the correct care and treatment.

The main cause:

To survive, you require insulin. It does a crucial task. It enables the blood glucose to feed your body by getting inside your cells. Even if you have diabetes type 2, your body continues to convert the carbohydrates in your food & drink into glucose. The pancreas subsequently releases insulin in response to this. However, since this insulin is unable to function correctly, the blood sugar levels continue to increase. More insulin is therefore released. This may gradually wear out the pancreas in certain type 2 diabetics, causing their bodies to produce less & less insulin. This puts you at risk for hyperglycemia and may result in even increased blood sugar levels. Having type 2 diabetes causes your insulin response to stop working properly. This results in the following:

- Your liver, muscles and fat (sometimes referred to as peripheral tissues) develop an inability to react to insulin, which prevents them from absorbing and using glucose.

- Your pancreas' beta cells run out of energy and are unable to make enough insulin.

Obesity:

The most common metabolic disorders are type 2 diabetes and obesity, so how you understand their matters. Despite being distinct conditions, they usually overlap. According to Caroline Apovian, MD, a specialist in nutrition and weight management, "Although lifestyle is essential for treating both obesity and diabetes, some people never become obese, and for those who do, lifestyle changes don't always work because obesity is indeed a disease & the body defends an increased body weight set point. The hormonal changes brought on by obesity might cause a patient to gain weight even after losing it. But type 2 diabetes and obesity are becoming more common. According to researchers, it's because of your surroundings. There is a greater selection of highly processed, high-fat meals available. Other "non-food things" are often present in these foods. These substances have been shown to alter how your bodies store fat & use energy by acting as endocrine disruptors. Even if there hasn't been enough research to establish a link, the majority of medical professionals and nutritionists advise against them.

Insulin resistance:

Type 2 diabetes is brought on by insulin resistance. However, it is possible to have insulin resistance while having no disease at all. Dr Chistofides says, "Diabetes is all about energy in & energy out." "There is a mishandling of how the body balances energy intake & energy demand in case of type 2 diabetes." This inefficient use of energy has an insulin resistance-causing sign of insulin insensitivity. If you consume a lot of processed meals with added sugar, your body will initially continue to release insulin as it attempts to absorb and utilise glucose. What may occur if you've prediabetes and consume too many sugary foods is as follows:

- Insulin sensitivity develops throughout time as a consequence of your peripheral tissues being less sensitive to the insulin released in excess amounts.

- Your sugar levels in the blood are still raised because your body isn't adequately absorbing and utilising glucose at this stage.

- Your pancreas' beta cells keep making and releasing insulin in an effort to control the sugar levels.

- When your beta cells are harmed and die, your body is unable to create enough insulin, which causes high blood sugar (hyperglycemia). The last sign of energy mismanagement is hyperglycemia, which is indicated by high haemoglobin A1C values and results in a type 2 diabetes diagnosis.

Diabetes type 2 symptoms:

Compared to type 1 diabetes, type 2 diabetes occurs more gradually. Many folks either don't experience any symptoms or are unaware of them. But you may observe:

- **Polydipsia:** It is an extreme case of thirst that is worse than what you experience on a hot day. You could have polydipsia if drinking doesn't satisfy it and your mouth often feels dry and cottony.

- **Hyperphagia:** In contrast to the hangry sensation you experience after missing meals, hyperphagia is an unrelenting hunger which is more bottomless. It may be hyperphagia if you've eaten a substantial, well-balanced meal (consider a dinner-sized plate), yet you still feel hungry afterwards.

- **Polyuria:** More frequent urination is referred to as polyuria. Based on your lifestyle, the drugs you're taking, & how much alcohol you consume, the frequency of toilet visits varies. However, peeing more than 7 ~ 8 times per day may be an indication of diabetes type 2.

- If you have diabetes type 2 and have not altered your exercise regimen or diet, weight loss may be a warning indication.

- Because blood sugar levels cause your eye lens to expand, blurred vision might appear quickly and can also come and go.

- Headaches may range in severity from mild to severe and might happen often.

- Given that yeast consumes sugar as food, having higher blood glucose levels may raise your chance of developing yeast infections.

- Extremity paresthesia, or tingling in the hands and feet, may resemble the feeling you experience when your foot "falls asleep" and may be an early indicator of diabetic neuropathy due to damage to your tiny blood vessels.

- The feeling of having a dry mouth is typically accompanied by an excessive amount of thirst.

- It takes more than being weary of being fatigued. You can be fatigued if you experience like you never get enough sleep, your body feels heavy, & even minor chores seem daunting. There may come a point when going from your room to the kitchen that seems like an Olympic sprint.

- Even the smoothest toothbrush may feel unpleasant when used to brush sore, irritated gums.

Risk factors associated with type 2 diabetes

There are certain factors that might raise your risk of developing type 2 diabetes. It's important to be mindful of these factors since type 2 diabetes symptoms aren't usually visible. They may consist of:

- **Age.** If you are white and over 40, or if you are a Black African, African Caribbean, or South Asian and over 25, you are more in danger.

- **Ethnicity.** Black African, African Caribbean, South Asian or Chinese ancestry puts you at higher risk.

- **Family background.** For instance, if your sibling, sister, parent, or you yourself have diabetes.

- **Medical background.** For instance, if you've got a history of severe mental illness, gestational diabetes, heart attacks, or strokes.

- If you are obese or overweight.

- If you have an excessively big waist.

Diabetic Type 1 vs Type 2 Differences: There are a few key distinctions between type 1 and type 2 diabetes:

- Diabetes type 1 is an autoimmune disorder. Type 1 diabetes cannot be cured; it can only be managed. Effective treatment and a change in lifestyle may reverse type 2 diabetes.

- In diabetes type 1, the pancreas is not able to make insulin, but in diabetes type 2, you can create less insulin, and your body responds to it less effectively.

- Without their insulin medication, people with type 1 diabetes risk death. Except in cases of severe pancreatic insufficiency, type 2 diabetics should refrain from receiving insulin therapy.

1.3 Managing Diabetes Type 2

Nobody like dieting, but, as Dr Apovian notes, "Weight decreases of as low as 3~5 per cent have been demonstrated to minimise the risk of diabetes type 2 in persons who've been medically recommended to lose weight. Dietary adjustments should include more fibre, more protein, healthier fats, fewer simple carbs, and fewer processed foods, as well as a reduction in calories and a change in the amount and quality of macronutrients. When medical professionals and nutritionists speak about inflammatory diets, they mostly refer to processed foods. Yet not just food has the potential to cause inflammation. A number of lifestyle choices may also cause systemic inflammation in your body, which can impair your ability to control your blood sugar levels. The following elements encourage systemic inflammation:

- packaged food
- extra sugars
- excessive alcohol consumption
- the inadequate amount and quality of sleep
- a few autoimmune diseases
- Smoking
- Anxiety and sadness

Although controlling diabetes type 2 is a matter of personal choice, you may follow some generic advice:

- Losing weight may enhance insulin sensitivity and lower blood glucose levels if your doctor recommends it for medical reasons.

- The Dietary Approach to Stop Hypertension (DASH) diet and the Mediterranean diet have been demonstrated to be useful in treating both diabetes & cardiovascular risk, yet there is no one ideal diet.

- Exercise. If you've never exercised before, start out slowly and build up your volume & intensity as your body becomes used to it. Strength and aerobic training together are the most effective forms of exercise for managing type 2 diabetes.

- Don't eat anything processed. Eat as little packaged food as you can. You'll often find the healthiest food in the grocery store's perimeter, so shop there.

- Make an effort to obtain adequate rest.

- If medication is necessary, consult with your physician to identify the dosage that is most effective for you.

Living with Type 2 Diabetes:

It's not necessary for type 2 diabetes to be a lifelong illness. On the other hand, the moment you are diagnosed with type 2 diabetes is the perfect time to start making changes to your lifestyle for the better. According to Dr Christofides, "What you do daily may make a difference." "Park at the far corner of the parking lot. Consider using the stairs. Think about eliminating packaged goods and just purchasing fresh foods. The optimal diabetes diet is subjective. Focus on balance and freshness. Include vegetables, whole grains, lean proteins (from meat or plants), nuts, legumes, seeds, and entire fruits in your diet.

- Be active. One of the most crucial things you really can do for your general health, including your mental well-being, is exercise. One of the greatest methods to maintain weight loss after losing it is via exercise.

- Find things you want to do and attempt to include friends and family in them. It's not necessary to exercise at a gym. Take a quick stroll in the neighborhood with a buddy, or go for a trek in the park. You'll get an added boost in health and happiness thanks to vitamin D.

1.4 Preventing Type 2 Diabetes ~ Role of a balanced diet

The idea of cutting up on the foods you like may feel overwhelming if you were just diagnosed with diabetes type 2 or if you were previously diagnosed with the disease but are now willing to make dietary changes. However, you may be glad to learn that maintaining a healthy diet for diabetes type 2 isn't as challenging as you might have thought, and you can still enjoy eating while managing this condition. Diabetes does not have a special diet. But the foods you consume also affect how good you feel & how much stamina you have, in addition to how you control your diabetes. An effective diabetes control strategy is built on the foundation of a balanced diet. Other pillars include managing stress, engaging in regular exercise, and taking any recommended medicines.

Balanced Diet & its Benefits:

Depending on the age, gender, level of activity, and objectives, you'll need to eat & drink differently. However, no one meal has all the vital elements your body needs. A healthy diet thus emphasizes diversity and consuming new items from each of major food categories each day. A balanced diet entails consuming more of certain things while consuming less of others. But while our dishes and bowls have become larger, portion sizes have increased recently. Additionally, eating bigger meals may make it harder for you to control your weight. We have additional details regarding maintaining a healthy weight for you. Below are the highlighted advantages of each food category. It's crucial for you to be aware of how certain foods may protect your heart while others have a more gradual effect on your blood sugar levels. Learn about them and how making healthy decisions may lower your chance of developing diabetic complications.

Veggies and fruits:

Diabetes does not exclude fruit consumption. Fruit and vegetables are naturally lower in calories and high in fibre, vitamins, and minerals. They also provide every meal flavour and diversity. Fresh, frozen, dry, and can all count. To receive the most variety of vitamins and minerals, choose a rainbow of colours. Fruit juices & smoothies should be avoided since they don't include as much fibre. You may be tempted to forgo fruit and vegetables if you're attempting to reduce the number of carbohydrates you consume. But it's crucial to incorporate them daily into your diet. You may experiment with lower-care choices. Fruits and vegetables may help prevent certain malignancies, high blood pressure, heart disease, and stroke, all of which are illnesses that are more likely to affect people with diabetes.

Benefits:

- maintain the health of your gut system
- aid in preventing heart disease, strokes, and several malignancies in the body

Aim for at least five meals each day for everyone. A piece is about equal to the size of your hand's palm.

Starchy foods:

Potatoes, pasta, rice, bread, naan, chapattis, and plantains are examples of starchy foods. All of them include carbohydrates, which are converted to glucose and utilized as fuel by your cells. Some starchy meals have the drawback of rapidly raising blood glucose levels, which might make it more difficult for you to control your diabetes. These foods have what is referred to as an increased glycemic index (GI).

There are certain starchy food alternatives that are healthier and have a more gradual impact on blood sugar levels. These include wholegrain bread, whole-wheat pasta, and basmati, brown, or wild rice, all of which have a low glycemic index (GI). Additionally, they have higher fibre, which supports healthy digestion. Therefore, if you want to reduce your carb intake, start by cutting down on foods like white bread, pasta, and rice.

Benefits:

- The fibre aids in maintaining a healthy digestive tract.
- some take longer to change your levels of blood sugar
- Whole grains safeguard your heart.

Make an effort to consume some starchy foods daily.

Foods high in protein include eggs, meat, fish, beans, almonds, and lentils:

Protein-rich foods like meat and fish help to maintain the health of your muscles. Less red & processed meat is necessary for a healthy diet since these meats have been connected to heart disease and cancer. Omega-3 oil, which is abundant in oily fish like salmon, mackerel, and sardines, may aid in protecting the heart.

Benefits:

- Keeps your muscles in good condition.
- Fish oil protects your heart.

Try to eat something from this category of food each day. Particularly, consume 1 or 2 servings of oily fish per week. You do not, however, have to consume meat every day.

Dairy products and substitutes:

Calcium and protein are abundant in milk, cheese, and yoghurt, which are wonderful for your bones, teeth, and muscles. However, certain dairy products are heavy in fat, especially saturated fat, so pick lower-fat substitutes.

In low-fat versions of dairy products like yoghurt, look for added sugar. If you need it sweeter, it's best to use unsweetened yoghurt & add some berries. If you prefer soy milk as a dairy substitute, choose one that is calcium-fortified and unsweetened.

Benefits:

- good for the teeth and bones
- prevents muscle deterioration

Every day, you need some calcium.

Oils & spreads:

While less saturated fat is necessary, you still need some fat in your diet. This is so that the risk of heart disease and stroke might be increased. Some saturated fats could raise blood cholesterol levels. Butter, palm nut oil, and coconut oil are some of these less healthful alternatives. Foods like vegetable oil, olive oil, rapeseed oil, spread prepared from these oils, & nut butter is examples of healthier saturated fats.

Benefits:

- Unsaturated fats support heart health.

1.5 Diabetic Diet

Simply keeping to regular mealtimes and consuming healthy foods in moderation constitutes a diabetic diet. A diabetic diet is a balanced, calorie- and fat-free eating regimen that is naturally high in nutrients. Fruits, vegetables, and whole grains are essential components. In actuality, a diabetic diet is the healthiest diet for the majority of people.

Creating a diabetic diet:

Your doctor will probably suggest that you see a nutritionist assist you in creating a healthy eating plan if you've diabetes or prediabetes. The plan assists you in managing your weight, controlling the risk factors of heart disease, including high blood pressure & blood fat levels, and controlling your blood glucose (sugar) levels. Extra calories & fat cause your blood sugar to spike, which is not what you want. If blood glucose levels aren't controlled, it may cause major issues, including high blood sugar (hyperglycemia), which, if it persists, may result in long-term concerns like nerve, kidney, and heart damage.

Making smart meal selections and keeping track of your eating patterns will help you maintain your blood glucose levels within a safe range. Weight reduction has a variety of additional health advantages, as well as making blood glucose management simpler for most persons with type 2 diabetes. A diabetic diet offers a well-planned, nourishing strategy to safely attain your goal if you want to reduce weight.

A diabetic diet is composed of:

- Eating 3 meals one day at regular intervals is the foundation of a diabetic diet. This improves how well you utilise the insulin your body makes or receives from a medicine.

- You may create a diet focused on your health objectives, preferences, and lifestyle with the assistance of a trained dietitian. Additionally, he or she may advise you on how to change your eating patterns, such as by picking portions that are appropriate for your size & level of exercise.

Suggested foods:

Use these nutrient-dense meals to make your calories count. Pick wholesome carbs and meals high in fibre, seafood, and "good" fats.

Nutritious carbs:

Simple carbohydrates like sugars and complex carbs like starches are broken down during digestion to produce blood glucose. Concentrate on wholesome carbs, like:

- Vegetables
- Fruits

- whole grains

- Beans, peas, and other legumes

- dairy goods with low fat, including milk & cheese

- Don't consume meals and beverages with extra fats, sweets, or salt, as well as less healthful carbs.

Foods high in fibre:

All plant food components that your body cannot digest or absorb are considered to be dietary fibre. Your body's digestion is moderated by fibre, which also helps to regulate blood sugar levels. Fibre-rich foods include:

- Vegetables

- Fruits

- Nuts

- Beans, peas, and other legumes

- whole grains

Heart-healthy fish

Eat seafood that is good for your heart at least 2 times a week. Omega-3 fatty acids, which are abundant in fish like salmon, tuna, mackerel, and sardines, may reduce heart disease.

Healthy fats:

Monounsaturated & polyunsaturated fatty acid-rich foods may aid in lowering your cholesterol levels. These consist of:

- Avocados

- Nuts

- Olive, peanut, and canola oils

- Don't go overboard, however, since fats all contain a lot of calories.

Foods to avoid:

Diabetes accelerates the formation of blocked & hardened arteries, increasing the risk of heart disease & stroke. The following ingredients may be detrimental to your efforts to maintain a healthy diet for your heart.

Saturated fats. Animal proteins, including butter, hot dogs, beef, sausage, & bacon, should be avoided, as should high-fat dairy products. Also, keep palm kernel and coconut oils to a minimum.

Tran's fats. Don't consume Trans fats, which are included in stick margarine, shortening, baked products, and processed snacks.

Cholesterol. Dairy products having high fat content, animal high-fat proteins, liver, egg yolks, & any other organ meat are all sources of cholesterol. Aim to consume not more than 200 mg of cholesterol every day.

Sodium. Limit your daily salt intake to 2,300 milligram or less. If you've high blood pressure, your doctor could advise you to set your sights even lower.

Putting everything together creates a strategy.

To assist you in maintaining a normal blood glucose level, you may develop a diabetic diet using a number of different strategies. You could discover that 1 or a combination of the following strategies works for you with the assistance of a dietitian:

1. The plate approach.

The ADA (Americans Diabetes Association) provides a straightforward meal-planning approach. Basically, it emphasizes eating more veggies. Take the following actions to prepare your plate:

- Nonstarchy veggies, such as carrots, spinach, and tomatoes, should make up half of your meal.

- Give a protein, like a lean pork, tuna, or chicken, a quarter of the dish.

- Add whole grains, like brown rice, or starchy vegetable, like green peas, to the final part of the plate.

- Include "healthy" fats in moderation, such as those found in avocados or nuts.

- Include a dish of dairy or fruit along with a glass of water, coffee or unsweetened tea.

2. Counting carbs.

Carbohydrates have the most effect on the blood glucose level since they break down into glucose. You may want to learn how to calculate the number of carbs you consume so that you can change the insulin dosage to assist in regulating your blood sugar. It's critical to monitor the carbohydrate content of each meal and snack.

You can learn portion control techniques from a nutritionist, who can also help you become a knowledgeable label reader. Additionally, you may learn from him or her how to pay close attention to portion size & carbohydrate content. A nutritionist may show you how to calculate the number of carbs in each meal and snack if you are taking insulin and how to change your insulin dosage appropriately.

3. Select your meals.

To assist you in making meal and snack plans, a nutritionist may suggest that you choose a certain food. A variety of foods are available for selection from lists that include sections for carbs, proteins, and fats.

"Choice" refers to one serving within a category. Serving each other item in that category contains about the same number of calories, protein, carbs, and fat as that meal option, as well as the same impact on blood sugar levels. For instance, selections on the starch, fruit, and milk list range from 12 ~ 15 grams of carbs.

4. Glucose index.

The glycemic index is used by some diabetics to choose meals, particularly carbs. This system places foods high in carbohydrates in order how affect blood sugar levels. Ask your dietician whether you think this approach would be effective for you.

Outcomes of a diabetic diet:

The easiest method to maintain control over your glucose level and avoid diabetic problems is to stick to your healthy eating plan. Additionally, you may modify it to meet your own objectives if you want to reduce weight.

A diabetic diet has additional advantages outside only helping you control your blood sugar. Following a diabetic diet is believed to lower the risk of cardiovascular illnesses and some forms of cancer since it suggests eating plenty of fruits, vegetables, and fibre. Additionally, eating low-fat dairy products may lower your future chance of having poor bone mass.

1.6 Antidiabetic Lifestyle

People who are more likely to develop diabetes & those who have already received a type 2 diagnosis are often urged to make lifestyle adjustments to assist in controlling their condition.

- Two and a half hours of moderate-intensity exercise or one hour and fifteen mins. of high-intensity exercise per week are the suggested lifestyle interventions.

- Progressive weight loss to reach a healthy BMI (body mass index).

- increasing consumption of vegetables & other meals rich in nutritional fibre, swapping refined carbs for whole-grain options

- lowering the consumption of saturated fat

Physical exercise: It is advised to engage yourself in either 2 and 1/2 hours of exercise of moderate intensity or 1 and 1/4 hours of vigorous exercise. Physical exercise with a moderate intensity includes:

- Rapid walking
- Cycling over a mostly level surface
- Aquatic exercise
- Hiking
- Rollerblading
- using a hand lawnmower

Among the vigorous physical activities are:

- Jogging
- swimming
- cycling at high speed or on an incline
- Football
- Gymnastics
- Skipping

It may be possible to refer certain patients for supervised or organized exercise sessions.

Loss of weight:

Overweight people should attempt to reduce weight gradually until they reach a healthy BMI. A healthy BMI is between:

- Ranging from 18.5 to 24.9
- Alternatively, for those of South Asian ancestry, between 18.5 & 22.9

Striving for progressive weight reduction with a goal of losing 5 to 10% of body weight over the course of a year is advised for those whose BMI is over the recommended limit. Losing weight may assist persons who already have type 2 diabetes or pre-diabetes better regulate their blood sugar levels and lower their chance of acquiring diabetes. Your doctor may recommend that you participate in an organized weight reduction program if your BMI is higher than 30. Orlistat is a weight reduction medication that may be recommended to those who are unable to lose weight via lifestyle modifications.

Stress:

It has been shown that stress increases the risk of type 2 diabetes. An individual's body triggers the threat response when they are under stress. Stress hormones are produced, raising blood pressure and blood sugar levels and activating the immune system, among other changes in the human body.

- Digestion, development, and other non-essential body processes are reduced so that energy may be utilized to combat or escape the danger that is triggering the threat response.

- Controlling blood sugar levels may be exceedingly challenging when someone is under constant stress, especially if they are unaware of their stress levels.

A straightforward, non-toxic method to regulate stress-related fluctuations in blood sugar is to use stress management strategies like mindfulness. The likelihood of acquiring complications associated with diabetes, like stroke, heart disease, hypertension, and mental health issues, including depression and anxiety, is also decreased by lowering stress levels.

1.7 Using an Air-Fryer ~ Diabetes-Friendly Cooking Equipment

The air fryer does not really fry the food; instead, it more closely resembles a countertop convection oven that has been improved. (However, keep in mind that baking and air-frying are two distinct processes.) This little appliance boldly asserts that it can simulate the results of deep-frying with just hot air and little or no oil at all. The popularity of this technology has increased over the past few years. Numerous meals, such as freshly baked cookies, roasted vegetables, homemade French fries, & frozen chicken wings, can be air-fried.

How an Air-fryer works:

The top part of the air fryer houses the heating element and fan. Hot air travels down and around the food you have put in the basket of the fryer when it is turned on. The food has a crisp texture akin to deep-frying without using oil because to the rapid circulation.

How to operate the air-fryer:

Put the food into the basket.

The basket's capacity may range from 2-10 quarts, depending on the size of your air fryer. To make the dish lovely and crispy, you usually need to add one to two tablespoons of the oil. To speed up cleaning, if you're pressed for time, use foil in the air fryer.

Establish the time & temperature.

Based on the thing you are preparing, air fryer cooking times & temperatures may vary from 5-25 mins at 350°-400°F.

Allow food to cook.

To ensure equal crisping, you can sometimes need to turn or flip the food midway while cooking. It's important to clean the equipment when you have finished cooking. Type-2 diabetes can be averted with the use of an air fryer. The cooking method used by air fryers is known as "air frying," and it doesn't utilize oil which is absorbed in the food. When an item is cooked in the air fryer, this may lower the fat level by up to 80%.

Using an Air-fryer to make a meal for a diabetic patient.

Air fryers are hailed as the healthy alternative to deep frying, & they are in many ways significantly healthier than deep fryers & many other methods of cooking. The main reason for this is that the air fryer can reduce the amount of fat in food by up to 80 percent by not using oil, and it also does a great job of preserving nutrients while cooking. You should monitor the amount of salt and fat you consume each day since too much of either may increase your risk of heart disease, high blood pressure, cholesterol, and blood sugar swings. A diabetic would thus profit from cooking in an air fryer since the amount of fat and salt may be reduced. Prepare dishes with the air fryer that are high in protein & vitamins.

You can prepare vegetables, beef, fowl, fish, nuts, soups, and more using an air fryer. In fact, many who choose to follow low-carb, "keto," & blood sugar diets have found the air fryer to be a useful tool. For making crispy French fries, whether frozen or freshly cooked potato cut fries, both air fryers & deep fryers are often utilized. However, you may get comparable effects using vegetables, more specifically: jimaca, celeriac, rutabaga, and zucchini, in place of French potato fries, which are high in carbs. Obesity and overweight have been demonstrated to raise the risk of diabetes type-2 and a wide range of other metabolic disorders. One must cut down on daily calorie consumption to stop the development of such disorders. An air fryer is a terrific tool for this project.

Foods that are deep fried have a high-fat content because they are cooked in hot oil, which is then absorbed into the meal throughout the cooking process. Less than half as many calories are included in each gram of fat (9 calories per gram compared to 4 calories for each gram of carbohydrate or protein). In certain situations, the air fryer may reduce food fat by up to 80%. Every meal prepared in an air fryer would have much fewer calories if the fat level were drastically reduced. Air-fried chicken wings have more protein than deep-fried chicken wings do. Except when it's deep-fried when it's truly fairly fat, chicken flesh is pretty lean meat.

With this in your mind, you may be able to see how using an air fryer might be advantageous for anybody attempting to get in shape or eat better, both of which are excellent strategies to stave against illnesses like type-2 diabetes.

Using the oil in an Air-fryer:

For diabetics, air fryers offer a contemporary substitute for conventional cooking techniques. Foods that are air-fried tend to be healthier since they cook rapidly and with little to no oil. An excellent technique to cook with fewer fat and calories is to use an air fryer. You can cook excellent food without fearing it drying out or burning on the base of the pan, thanks to its ability to distribute heat evenly.

One oil is known as rice bran oil. It is a good option for diabetics since it is high in monosaturated fatty acids, which lower cholesterol. Canola oil can be a wise option for diabetics, according to another study. The risk of cardiovascular illnesses has been shown to be lower when these oils are consumed. Other options are olive oil, coconut oil, avocado oil, and sunflower oil if you can't locate either of these. Olive oil's reputation as 1 of the healthiest oils for diabetics is another factor.

1.8 Overall Health Benefits of Using an Air fryer

When used correctly, air fryers provide a number of health advantages:

Losing weight may be aided by using air fryers.

Increased consumption of fried meals is directly linked to an increased risk of obesity. This is due to the fact that meals that are deep-fried often include a lot of fat and calories. Weight reduction is aided by converting to air-fried meals from deep-fried meals & by taking lesser harmful oils on a daily basis.

Air Fryer Reduces Calories.

Since they use a lot less oil than conventional fryers, air fryers also save calories. For instance, dishes that are air-fried may just need one tsp. of oil, which only contributes 40 calories. In comparison, using only one tbsp. of oil during deep-frying increases calorie content by roughly 120. So, switching from deep-fried to air-fried items may aid in weight control.

Compared to deep frying, air frying might be safer.

Foods are deep-fried by heating a big container of hot oil. This might be dangerous. Although air fryers do become hot, there's no chance of splashing, spilling, or unintentionally touching boiling oil. To guarantee safety, users should use frying appliances carefully and according to instructions.

The danger of hazardous acrylamide production is decreased by air fryers.

Food frying in oil may lead to the development of hazardous substances like acrylamide. When meals are cooked at high heat, such as when deep frying, this chemical develops in some of the foods. Acrylamide may be related to the emergence of several malignancies, including ovarian, endometrial, breast, pancreatic, and

esophageal cancer, as per the International Agency for the Research on Cancer. Although the findings are inconclusive, Trusted Sources have also shown a connection between dietary acrylamide & ovarian, endometrial, or kidney malignancies. People may reduce their risk of eating food containing acrylamide by shifting to air frying.

Reducing consumption of fried foods lowers illness risk.

Numerous harmful health issues have been linked too frequently using oil in cooking and eating traditional fried dishes. One may lessen their chance of developing these issues by using alternate cooking techniques for deep frying.

Chapter 2: Air Fried Diabetic Diet - Appetizers & Side Recipes

1. Coconut Shrimp

Ready in: 20 mins.

Serves: 4

Difficulty: easy

Ingredients:

- 2 beaten egg whites
- 1 lb. of (peeled & deveined) raw shrimp (large), 20 to 30 shrimp
- 1 tbsp. of water
- 1/4 cup of coconut flakes, unsweetened
- 1/2 cup of panko bread crumbs (whole-wheat)
- 1/2 tsp. of ground cumin
- 1/2 tsp. of ground coriander
- 1/2 tsp. of turmeric
- 1 cooking spray (nonstick)
- 1/8 tsp. of salt

Directions:

- Make use of paper towels to pat the shrimp dry. In a small bowl, mix the water and egg whites by whisking.
- In a separate small bowl, mix the coconut, panko bread crumbs, cumin, coriander, turmeric, and salt.
- The shrimp should be coated in the mixture of panko after being dipped in the egg mixture, letting any excess fall back into the bowl. The coated shrimp should be put on a wire rack. Repeat with all of the shrimp.
- Put the shrimp into the air fryer basket in a single layer. Spray nonstick cooking spray on the shrimp for two seconds. Air fried for 4 minutes at 205°C. Overturn the shrimp. Shrimp should be air-fried for two to four minutes or until golden brown. Serve hot.

Nutritional values per serving:

Total Calories: 180 kcal, **Fats:** 4.5 g, Carbohydrates: 9 g, **Protein:** 28 g

2. Fried Spicy Green Beans

Ready in: 20 mins.

Serves: 4

Difficulty: easy

Ingredients:

- 1 tbsp. of olive oil
- 1/2 oz. of green beans, fresh (trimmed)
- 1 tsp. of chilli garlic paste (Thai-style)
- 1/4 tsp. of salt
- 1 tbsp. of panko bread crumbs (whole-wheat)

Directions:

- Put green beans into a medium bowl and season with salt, panko bread crumbs, chile-garlic paste, and olive oil.
- Fill air fryer basket with the green beans. Set temperature up to 205°C & air fry for 3-4 minutes. Shake the basket of the air fryer. Add another 5-7 minutes to the air fryer. Serve hot

Nutritional values per serving:

Total Calories: 60 kcal, **Fats:** 4 g, **Carbohydrates:** 7 g, **Protein:** 2 g.

3. Sweet Potato Nachos

Ready in: 30 mins.

Serves: 4

Difficulty: medium

Ingredients:

- 1 sweet potato, medium (sliced in chips, 1/8-inch thick)
- 1 & 1/2 cup of the pepper-&-onion blend, frozen (partially thawed & drained)
- 1 cooking spray, nonstick
- 1 jalapeño pepper (cut lengthwise & seeded)

- 1/4 cup of salsa
- 1/4 cup of reduced-fat Mexican-style or cheddar cheese, shredded
- 2/3 cup of thinly sliced radishes
- 1/2 cup of romaine lettuce, shredded
- 4 cherry tomatoes (in fourths)
- 1 tbsp. of fresh cilantro, minced
- 2 tbsp. of light sour cream

Directions:

- Spread out the slices of sweet potato into the air fryer basket. Spray for one second with nonstick cooking spray. Over the potatoes, distribute the frozen veggies equally. Over the veggies, place the jalapeno skin side up. Spray for one second with nonstick cooking spray.

- Air-fried the potatoes for 20 mins, or until they are done, at a temperature of 190°C. They need to be crisp and delicate, not squishy. Jalapenos should be removed and placed in a bowl. Loosely cover with a kitchen towel, and let it stand for five minutes.

- Over the veggies, equally, distribute the cheese. Till the cheese is melted, air fried the food for two minutes.

- Remove the charred or browned peel off the jalapeno pepper with the point of a sharp knife. Peel and mince the pepper.

- Lift potatoes and veggies out of the air fryer basket using a spatula then spread them out evenly on a serving tray. The veggies should be covered with chopped jalapeno. Add the lettuce, tomatoes, radishes, and salsa on top. Add some cilantro and a spoonful of sour cream. Serve right away.

Nutritional values per serving:

Total Calories: 100 kcal, **Fats:** 3 g, **Carbohydrates:** 17 g, **Protein:** 4 g

4. Rosemary-Garlic Brussels sprouts
Ready in: 30 mins.

Serves: 4

Difficulty: medium

Ingredients:

- 2 minced garlic cloves
- 3 tbsp. of olive oil
- 1/2 tsp. of salt
- 1 pound of Brussels sprouts (halved), trimmed
- 1/4 tsp. of pepper
- 1-1/2 tsp. of fresh rosemary, minced
- 1/2 cup of panko bread crumbs

Directions:

- Set the air fryer up to 176°C. In a medium microwave-safe bowl, combine the first four ingredients. Microwave on high for 30 seconds.

- Add 2 tablespoons of the oil mixture and toss the Brussels sprouts. Place the Brussels sprouts onto a tray and cook for 4–5 minutes in an air fryer basket. Mix the sprouts. About 8 more minutes of simmering are needed to get the sprouts close to the desired level of softness. Stirring halfway during the cooking period.

- Toss remaining oil mixture, rosemary, & bread crumbs; sprinkle over sprouts. Cook for a further 3-5 minutes, or until the sprouts are tender and the crumbs are browned. Serve right away.

Nutritional values per serving:

Total **Calories:** 164 kcal, **Fats:** 11 g, **Carbohydrates:** 15 g, **Protein:** 5 g

5. Red Potatoes

Ready in: 20 mins.

Serves: 8

Difficulty: easy

Ingredients:

- 2 tbsp. of olive oil
- 2 pounds of small red potatoes (unpeeled), cut in wedges
- 1 tbsp. of minced rosemary (fresh) or 1 tsp. of dried crushed rosemary
- 1/2 tsp. of salt
- 2 cloves of garlic, minced
- 1/4 tsp. of pepper

Directions:

- Set air fryer up to 205°C. Put some oil on the potatoes. Toss lightly to coat after adding salt, rosemary, pepper, and garlic.
- Place in an air-fryer basket on an ungreased tray. Cook potatoes for 10 to 12 minutes, tossing once until they are golden brown & soft.

Nutritional values per serving:

Total Calories: 113 kcal, **Fats:** 1 g, **Carbohydrates:** 18g, **Protein:** 2 g.

6. Delicious Radishes

Ready in: 25 mins.

Serves: 6

Difficulty: easy

Ingredients:

- 3 tbsp. of olive oil
- 2-1/4 pounds of radishes, trimmed & quartered (about almost 6 cups)
- 1 tbsp. of fresh oregano (minced) or 1 tsp. of dried oregano
- 1/8 tsp. of pepper
- 1/4 tsp. of salt

Directions:

- Set air fryer up to 190°C. Toss the remaining ingredients with the radishes.
- Put the radishes in the air fryer basket on an oiled tray. Cook for 12 to 15 minutes, stirring periodically, until crisp-tender.

Nutritional values per serving:

Total Calories: 88 kcal, **Fats:** 7 g, **Carbohydrates:** 6 g, **Protein:** 1 g.

7. Breaded Summer Squash

Ready in: 25 mins.

Serves: 4

Difficulty: medium

Ingredients:

- 3 tbsp. of olive oil
- 4 cups of yellow summer squash, thinly sliced (3 medium)
- 1/2 tsp. of salt
- 1/8 tsp. of cayenne pepper
- 1/2 tsp. of pepper
- 3/4 cup of Parmesan cheese, grated
- 3/4 cup of panko bread crumbs

Directions:

- Set air fryer up to 176°C. Squash should be put in a big bowl. Season with oil and add; toss to coat.
- Combine cheese and bread crumbs in a small bowl. Squash should be dipped into the mixture of crumbs and patted to help the coating adhere. Squash should be arranged in one single layer in the air fryer basket on a tray in batches. Cook for approximately 10 minutes, or until the squash is soft and the coating is golden brown.

Nutritional values per serving:

Total Calories: 203 kcal, **Fats:** 14 g, **Carbohydrates:** 13 g, **Protein:** 6 g

8. Herb & Lemon Cauliflower

Ready in: 20 mins.

Serves: 4

Difficulty: easy

Ingredients:

- 4 tbsp. of olive oil, divided
- 1 head of cauliflower (medium), cut in florets (about almost 6 cups)
- 1/4 cup of fresh parsley, minced
- 1 tbsp. of fresh thyme, minced
- 1 tbsp. of fresh rosemary, minced
- 1 tsp. of lemon zest, grated
- 1/2 tsp. of salt
- 2 tbsp. of lemon juice
- 1/4 tsp. of red pepper flakes, crushed

Directions:

- Set the air fryer up to 176°C. Cauliflower & 2 tbsp. of olive oil are combined in a large bowl and coated. Cauliflower should be placed in one single layer in the air fryer basket on a tray in batches. Cook for 8 to 10 mins, stirring halfway through, or until the edges are browned, and the florets are soft. Add the remaining ingredients and 2 tablespoons of oil to a small bowl. Transferring the cauliflower to a big bowl, add the herb mixture and mix well.

Nutritional values per serving:

Total Calories: 161 kcal, **Fats:** 3 g, **Carbohydrates:** 14g, **Protein:** 8g

9. Air-Fried Asparagus

Ready in: 20 mins.

Serves: 4

Difficulty: easy

Ingredients:

- 4 tsp. of olive oil
- 1/4 cup of mayonnaise
- 1-1/2 tsp. of lemon zest, grated
- 1/2 tsp. of pepper
- 1 clove of garlic, minced
- 1/4 tsp. of seasoned salt
- 2 tbsp. of Parmesan cheese, shredded
- 1 pound of asparagus (fresh), trimmed
- Lemon wedges, optional

Directions:

- Set the air fryer up to 190°C. Combine the 1st 6 ingredients in a large bowl. Asparagus is added; toss to coat. Place in one single layer on the oiled tray in the air fryer basket while working in batches.
- Cook for 4-6 minutes, or until tender and gently browned. Sprinkle with some Parmesan cheese after transferring to a serving plate. Serve with lemon slices, if preferred.

Nutritional values per serving:

Total Calories: 156 kcal, **Fats:** 15 g, Carbohydrates: 3g, **Protein:** 2g

10. Green Tomato Stacks

Ready in: 35 mins.

Serves: 4

Difficulty: medium

Ingredients:

- 1/4 tsp. of lime zest, grated
- 1/4 cup of mayonnaise, fat-free
- 2 tbsp. of lime juice
- 1/2 tsp. of pepper, divided
- 1 tsp. of minced thyme (fresh) or 1/4 tsp. of dried thyme
- 1/4 cup of all-purpose flour
- 3/4 cup of cornmeal
- 2 egg whites (large), lightly beaten
- 1/4 tsp. of salt
- 2 red tomatoes (medium)
- 2 green tomatoes (medium)
- Cooking spray

- 8 slices of Canadian bacon, warmed

Directions:

- Set the air fryer up to 190°C. Refrigerate until serving. Combine lime zest, mayonnaise and juice, thyme, and 1/4 teaspoon pepper. Egg whites should be in a separate shallow bowl from the flour. Mix cornmeal, salt, and the last 1/4 teaspoon of pepper in a third bowl.

- Make four crosswise slices out of each tomato. Sprinkle some flour on each slice and shake off the excess. Toss in the cornmeal mixture, then dip in the egg whites.

- In the air-fryer basket, arrange tomatoes on a greased tray in batches and spritz with some cooking spray. Cook for 4-6 minutes, or until golden brown. Toss with cooking spray and turn. Cook for another 4-6 minutes, or until golden brown.

- Place 1 slice of each green tomato, bacon, and red tomato on top of each other for each serving. Eat with sauce.

Nutritional values per serving:

Total Calories: 114 kcal, **Fats:** 2 g, **Carbohydrates:** 18 g, **Protein:** 6 g

11. Air-Fried Roasted Green Beans
Ready in: 35 mins.

Serves: 6

Difficulty: medium

Ingredients:

- 1/2 pound of fresh mushrooms, sliced
- 1 pound of green beans (fresh), cut into pieces (2 inches)
- 1 red onion (small), halved & thinly sliced
- 1 tsp. of Italian seasoning
- 2 tbsp. of olive oil
- 1/8 tsp. of pepper
- 1/4 tsp. of salt

Directions:

- Set the air fryer up to 190°C. All ingredients should be combined and coated in a big bowl.

- Arrange the veggies in the air fryer basket on the oiled tray. Cook for 8–10 minutes, or until barely tender. Cook for a further 8 to 10 minutes, tossing to distribute until browned.

Nutritional values per serving:

Total Calories: 76 kcal, **Fats:** 5 g, **Carbohydrates:** 8g, **Protein:** 3g

12. Crispy bacon
Ready in: 8 mins.

Serves: 5

Difficulty: easy

Ingredients:

- 5 strips of bacon

Directions:

- Add bacon to the air fryer basket that has been heated to 190°C. Make an effort to layer it.

- Cook for 6-8 minutes, monitoring every few minutes to ensure the required amount of crispiness is reached.

- Add eggs if desired!

Nutritional values per serving:

Total Calories: 91 kcal, **Fats:** 8 g, **Carbohydrates:** 0 g, **Protein:** 2g

13. Air Fried Vegetables
Ready in: 30 mins.

Serves: 8

Difficulty: medium

Ingredients:

- 1 cup of broccoli florets
- 1/2 cup of baby carrots
- 1 cup of cauliflower florets
- 1/2 cup of sliced yellow squash
- 1/2 cup of sliced mushrooms

- 1/2 cup of sliced baby zucchini
- 1 small sliced onion
- 1 tbsp. of olive oil
- 1/4 cup of balsamic vinegar
- 1 tbsp. of minced garlic
- 1 tsp. of black pepper
- 1 tsp. of sea salt
- 1/4 cup of parmesan cheese
- 1 tsp. of red pepper flakes

Directions:

- Set the Air Fryer for three minutes at 200°C. Olive oil, garlic, salt, balsamic vinegar, pepper, & red pepper flakes should all be combined in a big bowl.

- Blend well. Vegetables are added; mix to combine. Fill the Air Fryer basket with veggies. For 8 minutes, cook.

- Cook veggies for a further 6 to 8 minutes after shaking them. Bake for 1 to 2 minutes after adding cheese.

Nutritional values per serving:

Total Calories: 61 kcal, **Fats:** 2 g, **Carbohydrates:** 7 g, **Protein:** 3 g

14. CrispyGarlic Croutons
Ready in: 20 mins.

Serves: 10

Difficulty: easy

Ingredients:

- 2 cups of Bread, half of loaf (200g)
- 2 tbsp. of Olive Oil
- 1 tbsp. of Marjoram
- 1/2 tbsp. of Garlic Powder

Directions:

- Ensure that the bread has cooled. Slice it into squares, then the same-sized slices. Put all the croutons in a large bowl large enough to include all of the herbs & oil.

- Add marjoram, dry garlic, and oil. Completely combine all the croutons using a large spatula. Ensure sure the oil & herbs are distributed evenly.

- Put as many of your Croutons as your Air Fryer will hold. If you add more than one layer, they won't crisp up completely.

- Turn on the air fryer. Since you previously covered your Croutons with oil, you don't need to add any more.

- You must use the temperature settings you're used to for your Air fryer.

- The Crunchy Croutons are set to be served after 10 minutes. Serve them warm or hot, or allow them to cool. Everything depends on how you want to utilize them.

Nutritional values per serving:

Total Calories: 50 kcal, **Fats:** 4g, **Carbohydrates:** 1 g, **Protein:** 2g

15. Air Fried Cabbage
Ready in: 15 mins.

Serves: 4

Difficulty: easy

Ingredients:

- 1 head of cabbage
- 1 tsp. of sea salt
- 2 tbsp. of olive oil
- 1 tbsp. of Old Bay Garlic and Herb seasoning
- 1 tsp. of ground pepper (fresh)

Directions:

- Divide the cabbage into quarters, then insert the pie-shaped pieces into the air fryer.

- Sprinkle olive oil all over the cabbage segments. On the cabbage, season with salt, pepper, and Old Bay.

- Do 5 minutes of air frying at 190°C. Use tongs to toss the cabbage; the pieces will separate into big bits.

- Do 3–4 extra minutes of air frying

Nutritional values per serving:

Total Calories: 105 kcal, **Fats:** 7 g, **Carbohydrates:** 10g, **Protein:** 2g

16. Jalapeño Bacon Wrapped Poppers
Ready in: 25 mins.

Serves: 6

Difficulty: easy

Ingredients:

- 6 jalapeño peppers
- 12 uncured bacon slices, not thick cut
- 4 ounces cream cheese, at normal temperature
- ⅓ cup of shredded cheddar cheese
- Ranch Dressing to dip, (Optional)
- ½ tsp. of garlic powder

Directions:

- Remove the seeds & ribs by lengthwise slicing each jalapeno pepper in half. Wash the hands before continuing.
- Garlic powder, shredded cheddar, and cream cheese should all be mixed together in a bowl.
- To make things simpler, use a little silicone spatula to spoon the filling into each side of the jalapeno pepper.
- Take 1/2 to 3/4 of a bacon slice and tie it around each pepper, according to the size of the peppers. To enable you to tuck the ends in, start at the bottom. Make sure you have lots of bacon rolled around and terminating beneath the pepper and that you wrap them pretty tightly. By doing this, the filling won't be exposed, and the bacon won't shrivel up and seep out.
- Place them on the air fryer's wire racks; use six per rack and bake them at 185°C for 15 minutes. Bake for a further 3 to 4 minutes, or till the bacon is crisp, at 200°C.
- Present them warm, with the option of dipping them in ranch dressing.

Nutritional values per serving:

Total Calories: 125 kcal, **Fats:** 9 g, **Carbohydrates:** 2g, **Protein:** 5 g

17. Air-Fried Okra
Ready in: 35 mins.

Serves: 8

Difficulty: medium

Ingredients:

- ½ cup of all-purpose flour
- 1 tsp. of garlic powder
- ¼ cup of cornmeal
- 2 eggs (large), lightly beaten
- 8 ounces of okra pods (fresh), halved lengthwise
- 1 tbsp. of water
- Cooking spray
- ½ tsp. of Cajun seasoning (Optional)
- ½ tsp. of kosher salt, divided
- ½ cup of mayonnaise
- 2 tbsp. of ketchup
- 2 tbsp. of fresh chives, chopped
- 1 tsp. of Worcestershire sauce
- 1 tsp. of hot sauce

Directions:

- Set the air fryer up to 200°C and wait five minutes. Garlic powder, cornmeal, and flour are combined on a small plate. In one separate shallow dish, combine the eggs and water. Okra is dipped in the egg mixture, then dredged in the mixture of flour, and the excess is shaken off.
- Spread a good amount of frying spray over the okra and place half of it evenly in the fryer basket. Cook for about 10 mins, shaking the container halfway through, then coat with cooking spray once more. Place the salt on a dish once you've transferred the okra there with the rest of the okra & 1/4 tsp. Salt, repeat the

process. If desired, evenly distribute Cajun spice over the okra.

- In the meanwhile, mix the mayonnaise, chives, Worcestershire, ketchup, and spicy sauce into a small bowl. Serve the sauce beside the okra.

Nutritional values per serving:

Total Calories: 150 kcal, **Fats:** 11 g, **Carbohydrates:** 11 g, **Protein:** 2 g

18. Crispy Chickpeas

Ready in: 20 mins.

Serves: 4

Difficulty: medium

Ingredients:

- 1 can of unsalted chickpeas (15 ounces), rinsed & drained
- ¼ tsp. of smoked paprika
- 1 ½ tbsp. of toasted sesame oil
- ¼ tsp. of crushed red pepper
- Cooking spray
- ⅛ tsp. of salt
- 2 wedges of lime

Directions:

- Cover several layers of the paper towels with chickpeas. Roll the chickpeas beneath the paper towels for drying them on all sides, then add additional paper towels on top and pat until extremely dry.

- In a medium bowl, combine chickpeas & oil. Salt, crushed red pepper, and paprika should be added. Pour into a cooking spray-coated air fryer basket. Cook for 12 to 14 minutes at 205°C, shaking the basket regularly until very nicely browned. Serve the chickpeas with lime wedges on top.

Nutritional values per serving:

Total Calories: 132 kcal, **Fats:** 5.4g, **Carbohydrates:** 14 g, **Protein:** 4.7 g

19. Air-Fried Zucchini

Ready in: 30 mins.

Serves: 4

Difficulty: medium

Ingredients:

- 2 tbsp. of Parmesan cheese, grated
- ½ tsp. of dried oregano
- 1 tbsp. of extra-virgin olive oil
- ½ tsp. of salt
- ¼ tsp. of onion powder
- ¼ tsp. of garlic powder
- ¼ tsp. of ground pepper
- 2 large zucchini (8-ounce), sliced into 1/4-inch thick pieces
- ⅛ tsp. of crushed red pepper
- Lemon wedges, to serve
- 2 tsp. of lemon juice

Directions:

- Set the air fryer up to 205°C and wait five minutes. In a medium bowl, combine the Parmesan, oregano, oil, salt, pepper, onion powder, garlic powder, and crushed red pepper. Add the zucchini and combine.

- Place the slices of zucchini in one single layer into the fryer basket, working in batches if required. Cook for 10 to 12 minutes, turning once, until golden brown. Lemon wedges should be served with lemon juice.

Nutritional values per serving:

Total Calories: 64 kcal, **Fats:** 5 g, **Carbohydrates:** 5 g, **Protein:** 2 g

20. Air-Fried Plantains

Ready in: 55 mins.

Serves: 4

Difficulty: medium

Ingredients:

- 2 ripe plantains, medium (about 1 and 1/4 pounds), peeled & sliced (1/2 inch)
- ¼ tsp. of salt
- 2 tbsp. of avocado oil, divided

Directions:

- For 10 minutes, preheat the air fryer to 182°C. Spray frying oil on the fryer basket liberally. In a medium dish, combine plantains with 1 tbsp. Oil. Place the plantains into the fryer basket in a single layer, working in batches if required. Cook for 5 minutes, then turn the plantains and cook for an additional 6 to 8 minutes, or until they are well-browned and crispy. Transfer plantains with caution to a chopping board.

- Flatten each slice of plantain into a disk approximately 1/4-inch thick using the flat base of a small dish or pan; transfer to a larger bowl. Mix the remaining 1 tbsp. oil with the mashed plantains. Return the plantains to the fryer basket in a single layer, working in batches if required. Cook for 5 to 7 minutes, until certain areas are crisp. Serve right after adding salt.

Nutritional values per serving:

Total Calories: 171 kcal, **Fats:** 7 g, **Carbohydrates:** 29 g, **Protein:** 1g

21. Air-Fried Carrots

Ready in: 20 mins.

Serves: 6

Difficulty: easy

Ingredients:

- 1 pound of carrots (small), peeled & cut lengthwise in half
- 1 tbsp. of olive oil
- 2 tbsp. of Parmesan cheese, grated
- 2 tsp. of brown sugar
- ½ tsp. of smoked paprika
- 1 tsp. of dried tarragon
- ¼ tsp. of ground pepper
- ½ tsp. of salt

Directions:

- Set the air fryer up to 205°C and wait five minutes. Spray some cooking spray on the frying basket lightly.

- In a medium bowl, combine the carrots, oil, Parmesan, brown sugar, paprika, tarragon, salt, and pepper; toss to combine. Add carrots to the basket of the fryer and cook for 6 minutes; if required, work in batches. For a further 6 minutes, sauté the carrots on the other side until they are soft and golden.

Nutritional values per serving:

Total Calories: 68 kcal, **Fats:** 3 g, **Carbohydrates:** 9 g, **Protein:** 1 g

22. Air-Fried Eggplant

Ready in: 50 mins.

Serves: 8

Difficulty: easy

Ingredients:

- 2 eggplants (small), sliced in 1/4-inch thick
- ¼ cup of all-purpose flour
- ½ tsp. of salt
- 2 eggs (large), lightly beaten
- ¼ cup of Parmesan cheese (grated), plus some more for garnish
- ½ cup of panko breadcrumbs, whole-wheat
- 1 ½ tsp. of Italian seasoning
- 1 tbsp. of chopped fresh parsley
- Cooking spray, Olive oil

Directions:

- Salt the slices of eggplant equally, then set aside for 10 minutes. With a paper towel, dry the eggplant slices.

- Cover a shallow dish with flour. Put the eggs in a separate, small dish. In a third shallow dish, mix the panko, Parmesan, and Italian seasoning together. Slices of eggplant should be dredged in flour, then dipped in egg, excess shaken off, and finally dredged in panko mixture.

- Set the air fryer up to 182°C. Spread frying spray liberally over the eggplant slices and arrange half of them in an equal layer in the fryer basket. Cook for 5 to 6 minutes, or until brown and crispy on one side. Cook the eggplant slices for 5 to 6 minutes, flipping them halfway through until they are golden and crispy. Place on a platter. With the remaining slices of eggplant, repeat the process. Add some parsley and more Parmesan for garnish, if preferred.

Nutritional values per serving:

Total Calories: 53 kcal, **Fats:** 2 g, **Carbohydrates:** 8 g, **Protein:** 3 g

---

23. Blooming Onions
Ready in: 35 mins.

Serves: 8

Difficulty: medium

Ingredients:

- Cooking spray

- 2 eggs (large)

- 2 large sweet onions (12-ounce)

- ½ cup of low-fat milk

- 1 tsp. of paprika, divided

- ¼ cup of whole-wheat flour

- ½ tsp. of garlic powder

- ½ tsp. of salt, divided

- ½ tsp. of onion powder

- 1 cup of panko breadcrumbs

- ¼ tsp. of cayenne pepper, divided

- 2 tbsp. of cocktail sauce

- ½ cup of mayonnaise

Directions:

- For five minutes, preheat the air fryer to 190°C. Spray cooking spray on the fryer basket.

- Remove the onion's stem end and peel it. On a cutting board, arrange the onions root-side down. Make 16 slices by cutting through each of the onions, stopping 1/4 inch just above the roots.

- In a medium bowl, combine the eggs, flour, milk, and 1/2 tsp. Paprika, 1/4 tsp. Salt, 1/8 tsp. Cayenne, garlic and onion powders. In another medium dish, add the breadcrumbs.

- Dredge each onion into the breadcrumbs to fully coat it after dipping it in the batter and letting the excess drip off. (During the dredging operation, pull onion "petals" apart frequently to ensure that batter and breadcrumbs are entering every crevice.) After spraying the basket with cooking spray, add the onions. Cook for 20-25 minutes or until crispy. Finish by adding the last 1/4 tsp. of salt.

- In the meanwhile, combine the remaining 1/2 tsp. Paprika, 1/8 tsp. Cayenne, cocktail sauce, and mayonnaise in a small dish. Along with the dipping sauce, serve the onions.

Nutritional values per serving:

Total Calories: 170 kcal, **Fats:** 11g, **Carbohydrates:** 15g, **Protein:** 3 g

24. Air-Fried Broccoli

Ready in: 25 mins.

Serves: 4

Difficulty: medium

Ingredients:

- 1 medium head of broccoli (14-ounce), trimmed & cut into bite-size florets
- 2 tbsp. of olive oil
- ¼ cup of Parmesan cheese, grated
- 1 tsp. of garlic powder
- 1 lemon wedge
- ¼ tsp. of ground pepper

Directions:

- For five minutes, preheat the air fryer to 190°C. In a large bowl, combine the broccoli, oil, Parmesan, garlic powder, and pepper. Stir to combine.
- Place the broccoli into the fryer basket in a single layer, working in batches if required. Cook for 5 to 7 minutes, or until crisp and tender. Before serving, transfer to the serving dish & squeeze a lemon slice over the top.

Nutritional values per serving:

Total Calories: 105 kcal, **Fats:** 9 g, **Carbohydrates:** 5 g, **Protein:** 4 g

25. Air-Fried Spaghetti Squash

Ready in: 25 mins.

Serves: 4

Difficulty: easy

Ingredients:

- 1 tbsp. of olive oil
- ½ tsp. of kosher salt
- 1 spaghetti squash, small (2 pounds), halved & seeded
- ¼ tsp. of ground pepper

Directions:

- For five minutes, preheat the air fryer to 190°C.

- Apply oil to the squash's flesh and season it with salt & pepper. Place the squash into the fryer basket with the skin side down and cook for approximately 18 minutes, working in batches if required.
- Squash should be taken out of the air fryer. With a fork, shred the flesh & transfer it to a serving plate.

Nutritional values per serving:

Total Calories: 82 kcal, **Fats:** 4 g, **Carbohydrates:** 11 g, **Protein:** 1 g

Chapter 3: Air Fried Diabetic Diet - Beef Recipes

1. Italian-Style Beef Meatballs
Ready in: 45 mins.

Serves: 12

Difficulty: medium

Ingredients:

- 1 shallot (medium), minced (almost about two tbsp.)
- 2 tbsp. of olive oil
- 3 cloves of garlic, minced (almost about 1 tbsp.)
- 2 tbsp. of whole milk
- 1/4 cup of panko crumbs (whole-wheat)
- 2/3 pound of lean ground beef
- 1 egg (large), lightly beaten
- 1/3 pound of bulk turkey sausage
- 1/4 cup of flat-leaf parsley, fresh (finely chopped)
- 1 tbsp. of fresh thyme, finely chopped
- 1 tbsp. of fresh rosemary, finely chopped
- 1 tbsp. of Dijon mustard
- 1/2 tsp. of kosher salt

Directions:

- Set the air fryer up to 200°C. Over medium-high heat, preheat the oil into a medium nonstick pan. Add the shallot and sauté for 1 to 2 minutes, or until soft. Add the garlic and simmer for approximately one minute, until fragrant. Remove from heat.
- Combine panko & milk in a big bowl. Allow standing for five minutes.
- Combine panko mixture with meat, turkey sausage, parsley, egg, rosemary, mustard, thyme, salt, and sautéed shallot and garlic. Gently blend by stirring.
- Form the mixture into 1 & 1/2-inch balls with care. Put the formed balls in the air fryer basket in a single layer. Half the meatballs should be cooked for 10 to 11 minutes at 200°C until they are just barely browned and done. Get rid of it and stay warm. The remaining meatballs, and repeat.
- You may serve the warm meatballs with the toothpicks as an appetizer or as a main meal with rice, pasta, or spiralized zoodles.

Nutritional values per serving:

Total Calories: 122 kcal, **Fats:** 8 g, **Carbohydrates:** 0 g, **Protein:** 10 g

2. Air Fried Meatloaf
Ready in: 45 mins.

Serves: 6

Difficulty: easy

Ingredients:

- 2 eggs (large)
- 2 pounds of ground beef (80/20)
- 1/4 cup of milk
- 1 packet of meatloaf seasoning (1.5 ounces)
- 2/3 cup of Italian breadcrumbs
- 1 tbsp. of Worcestershire sauce

For topping:

- 1/2 cup of light brown sugar
- 1 cup of ketchup
- 1/2 tbsp. of Worcestershire sauce
- 1 tbsp. Of Dijon mustard

Directions:

- Set your air fryer's thermostat to 182°C.
- In a large bowl, mix together the eggs, beef, milk, meatloaf seasoning, bread crumbs, and Worcestershire sauce. You may just use your hands or a large spoon.
- Shape it into a loaf, then set it into the air fryer.
- It needs 25 minutes to cook.

- Combine the brown sugar, ketchup, Dijon mustard, & Worcestershire sauce into a small bowl while the meatloaf cooks.

- Place 1/4 cup of topping mix on the meatloaf after 25 minutes. It should reach 67°C after 5-10 minutes of further cooking in the air fryer.

- Take the meatloaf out of the air fryer, put more ketchup mixture on top, and serve.

Nutritional values per serving:

Total Calories: 189 kcal, Fats: 9 g, Carbohydrates: 13g, Protein: 14 g

3. Cheeseburger Pockets
Ready in: 12 mins.

Serves: 4

Difficulty: easy

Ingredients:

- 1 lb. of Beef (Ground), Cooked and Drained

- 1 can of Biscuit dough (8 Count)

- Sharp Shredded Cheddar Cheese

Directions:

- Take the biscuits out from the can & roll or flatten the dough with your hands to make it as thin as possible.

- Four of the flattened biscuits should be topped with a piece of ground meat and shredded cheddar cheese.

- Top the biscuit with the meat and cheese with another biscuit that hasn't been topped. Pull the dough into a pocket until it is completely enclosed.

- Seal the edges by pressing a fork down on edge.

- As many pockets as will fit should be placed in oiled air fryer baskets.

- Once inside the air fryer, if preferred, coat with the olive oil cooking spray before air frying for 4-5 minutes at 185°C.

- After the timer sounds, gently flip the pockets over.

- Air Fry for 4-5 more minutes at 185°C. Given that every air fryer heats differently check on them after three to four minutes.

- When finished, they will become well browned.

Nutritional values per serving:

Total Calories: 382 kcal, Fats: 24g, Carbohydrates: 7 g, Protein: 33 g

4. Air Fried Hamburgers
Ready in: 23 mins.

Serves: 4

Difficulty: medium

Ingredients:

- ½ tsp. of salt

- 1 pound of ground beef (lean), 80/20

- ½ tsp. of onion powder

- ½ tsp. of pepper

- ¼ cup of barbecue sauce, optional

- ¼ tsp. of garlic powder

For serving:

- 4 buns of hamburger

- Toppings, as desired

Directions:

- In a medium bowl, combine the meat, pepper, salt, onion powder, & garlic powder.

- Make 4 patties that are approximately 1/2" thick. With your thumb, press a tiny hole into the centre of the patties. If using barbecue sauce, brush it on the patties.

- Set the air fryer's temperature to 187°C. Add patties to the basket in a single layer.

- Cook for six minutes. When the meat reaches 67°C, flip the burger over & cook for an additional 3–5 minutes.

- Cook for another minute after adding cheese, if using. Put on buns.

Nutritional values per serving:

Total Calories: 365 kcal, **Fats:** 19 g, Carbohydrates: 22 g, **Protein:** 25 g

5. Crispy Empanadas
Ready in: 27 mins.

Serves: 8

Difficulty: easy

Ingredients:

- 1 bell pepper, diced
- 1 lb. of ground beef
- 1 packet (1 oz.) of taco seasoning
- 1 package of pie crusts, refrigerated (2 crusts total), at room temperature
- 1/4 cup of water or beef broth
- 1/2 cup of cheese shredded
- 1 whisked egg
- 1/2 diced onion

Directions:

- Cook the ground beef, green and red peppers, & onions in a medium skillet over medium heat until the ground beef gets browned and the onions are translucent.
- Add water and taco seasoning; stir. Take the food off the stove and let it cool.
- Lay out the pie crust on a surface that won't stick. Take one of the pie crusts, and using a round cup or bowl (one with a 5-inch diameter works great), cut out 3 circles from it.
- Combine the leftover dough and roll it out to a thickness that is comparable to the original crust. Circle-cut a fourth one. The second pie crust should be processed similarly for a total of 8 pieces.
- Spoon a couple of teaspoons of the beef mixture over each circle after it has cooled, then top with cheese. Each dough circle should be folded in half, and the edges should be sealed with a little water. Edges may be pressed using a fork.

- Brush each empanada with the beaten egg. Four at a time, place empanadas in the oiled air fryer basket. Heat the air fryer to 182°C for five minutes.
- Cook for 5-7 minutes at 182°C or until the tops are as browned as you want. Serve with your preferred toppings, such as lettuce, sour cream, tomatoes, salsa, and guacamole.

Nutritional values per serving:

Total Calories: 189 kcal, **Fats:** 14 g, Carbohydrates: 2g, **Protein:** 13 g

6. Taco Pie
Ready in: 30 mins.

Serves: 4

Difficulty: medium

Ingredients:

- 1 onion, diced
- 1 tbsp. of oil
- 8 oz. of protein, ground (vegetarian, ground beef substitute etc.)
- ½ cup of corn kernels
- 1 tbsp. of taco seasoning
- ½ cup of Bisquick
- 2 eggs
- 1 cup of milk
- 1 cup of chopped lettuce
- 1 cup of cheddar cheese, shredded
- 1.5 cup of tomatoes (fresh), diced

Directions:

- Heat the oil in a pan over medium heat, add the onion, & sauté for 3 minutes more before adding the protein and cooking it through.
- Corn and spices may then be added. To blend, stir.
- Whisk the Bisquick, milk, and eggs in a small bowl. Add to the pan mixture.

- Fill the air fryer pot that is oiled with the whole skillet mixture. For 16-minute air fry at 190°C. At the ten-minute mark, stir.

- Add cheese and continue to air fry for 3 minutes.

- Add lettuce and chopped tomatoes on top. Enjoy!

Nutritional values per serving:

Total Calories: 403 kcal, **Fats:** 22g, **Carbohydrates:** 28g, **Protein:** 25 g

7. Beef & Bean Taquitos
Ready in: 25 mins.

Serves: 20

Difficulty: easy

Ingredients:

- 1 Package of Regular or Gluten-Free Taco Seasoning

- 1 Pound of Ground Beef

- 1 can of Refried Beans

- 20 Tortillas (White Corn)

- 1 Cup of Sharp Cheddar, Shredded

Directions:

- If the ground beef hasn't been prepared yet, start by doing so.

- According to the directions on the box, brown the meat over medium-high heat before adding the taco seasoning.

- When you are through with the meat, microwave the tortillas for approximately 30 seconds to soften them.

- Spray non-stick cooking spray on a layer of foil or add it to the air fryer basket.

- Each tortilla should be topped with cheese, beans, and ground meat.

- Wrap them firmly and put them into the air fryer seam side down.

- Add a little mist of oil spray, preferably one containing olive oil.

- Cook for 12 minutes at 200°C. Repeat with any extra tortillas.

Nutritional values per serving:

Total Calories: 181 kcal, **Fats:** 9 g, **Carbohydrates:** 14g, **Protein:** 11 g

8. Lamb Meatball Kebabs
Ready in: 35 mins.

Serves: 8

Difficulty: medium

Ingredients:

- 1 pound of ground lamb

- 1 pound of ground beef

- 1 onion (small), diced finely

- 1/4 cup of parsley (fresh), chopped

- 2 cloves of garlic, minced

- 2 tsp. of cumin

- 1 tsp. of allspice

- 1 1/2 tsp. of salt

- 1/2 tsp. of paprika

- 1/2 tsp. of nutmeg

- 1/4 tsp. of black pepper

- 1/4 tsp. of cinnamon

Directions:

- In a food processor, combine all the ingredients and process until smooth.

- Form the beef mixture into kebab-like patties by dividing it into equal parts (or any other shape you like).

- Fill the basket of the air fryer with kebabs. Avoid overlapping. Based on the size of the air fryer, you may have to cook the meatballs in batches.

- Cook for 12 minutes at 195°C, rotating once.

Nutritional values per serving:

Total Calories: 238 kcal, **Fats:** 6 g, **Carbohydrates:** 1g, **Protein:** 22 g

9. Zucchini Filled With Hamburger
Ready in: 22 mins.

Serves: 6

Difficulty: easy

Ingredients:

- 1 pound of ground beef
- 3 Zucchinis
- 1 cup of tomato sauce
- 1 tbsp. of Italian Seasoning, in half
- Salt & black Pepper
- 1 tbsp. of Garlic, minced
- Olive Oil Cooking Spray
- 1 Cup of Mozzarella, grated

Directions:

- Wash and pat dry zucchini gently.
- Remove the zucchini's stem, then cut each one in half lengthwise.
- To form a boat-shaped container for the ground beef, use a spoon to scoop out the inside of the zucchini seeds.
- Season the zucchini well with salt & pepper. Add a half-teaspoon of Italian seasoning next.
- Spray the small casserole dish that is appropriate for air frying inside and out. As an alternative, air fry the zucchini on foil.
- In a skillet over medium heat, brown the beef with the garlic, 1/2 tsp. Italian seasoning, and salt and pepper. Tomato sauce should be added when the steak begins to brown.
- After thoroughly combining, simmer the meat for a further 3 minutes to fully integrate the sauce.
- Pour the ground beef into the prepped zucchini boats at that point.
- Sprinkle freshly grated mozzarella over the ground meat.
- Insert a casserole dish or the basket of air fryer basket into which the zucchini boats will fit. There could be a need for two batches, based on the size of your air fryer.
- The zucchini boats are air-fried for 10 minutes at 182°C.
- Serve warm.

Nutritional values per serving:

Total Calories: 312 kcal, **Fats:** 20 g, **Carbohydrates:** 7 g, **Protein:** 26 g

10. Beef Meatball Wraps
Ready in: 35 mins.

Serves: 8

Difficulty: medium

Ingredients:

- ¼ cup of mint (fresh), finely chopped
- 1 ½ cups of plain Greek yoghurt.
- 3 tbsp. of lemon juice, freshly squeezed
- ½ tsp. of salt divided
- 3 minced cloves of garlic, divided
- ½ tsp. of pepper divided
- 1 lb. of ground lamb
- 1 lb. of lean beef (ground), 92% lean
- ¾ cup of English cucumber seeded & shredded
- ½ cup of thinly sliced red onion
- 1 tomato (large), sliced
- 8 Greek flatbreads
- 3 cups of shredded lettuce

Directions:

- Peel, slice and use a spoon to remove the cucumber's seeds. Cucumber should be finely chopped and put into a dish or sieve. While you make the sauce, set them aside.
- Combine yoghurt, mint, 2 minced cloves of garlic, lemon juice, 1/4 teaspoon salt, and 1/4 tsp. Pepper in a medium bowl.

- While assembling the meatballs, divide 1/3 cup of the yoghurt mixture, cover the remaining sauce, and chill.

- Combine the ground beef, lamb, 1 minced clove of garlic, remaining salt, pepper, and 1/3 cup yoghurt mixture into a large mixing dish. Knead the ingredients with your hands until it is well blended. To properly operate the mixture and combine it.

- Using a food scale, divide the mixture into eight 4-ounce balls, which you should then form into 5-inch cylinders. Place the meatballs on the rack of the air fryer, spacing them apart to allow for optimum air circulation, and coat the basket with nonstick spray. You may have to do this in 2 batches if you've got a small appliance.

- Preheat the air fryer to 205°C. Cook for 7-8 minutes, turn and cook for an additional 4-6 minutes, or until cooked through and lightly browned. The internal temperature of the meat should be 67°C.

- Combine the Greek yoghurt sauce with the strained, finely chopped cucumber.

- Top the meatball with tomato, lettuce, red onion, and yoghurt sauce on the Greek flatbread.

Nutritional values per serving:

Total Calories: 277 kcal, **Fats:** 16 g, **Carbohydrates:** 5 g, **Protein:** 26 g

11. Manwich Air-Fried Sloppy Joe Bombs
Ready in: 40 mins.

Serves: 16

Difficulty: medium

Ingredients:

- 1 can of Manwich
- 1 lb. of ground beef
- 1 can of flakey biscuits
- 1 egg
- 1 cup of mozzarella cheese

Directions:

- Brown the ground meat in a medium skillet.

- After draining the fat, add the Manwich can and stir. Let the meat cool fully. For leftovers, try this recipe.

- Use a rolling pin or your hands to press the biscuit dough into a flat surface.

- Place around 2 tbsp. of cheese in the dough's middle. Mix cheese by hand into the dough

- Meanwhile, sprinkle 1/4 cup or so of the mixture of meat over the mozzarella.

- Close the sides by pinching them together, taking care not to get sauce on the dough.

- After that, roll a little in your palm before putting it in the basket or on the sprayed Air Fryer tray.

- Apply the egg wash by brushing.

- After flipping, cook for a further 8 minutes in an air fryer that has been prepared to 190°C.

- Perform one last flip, then cook for an additional 4 minutes, or till golden brown & the inside is no longer doughy.

- Give it five minutes to settle and cool before serving.

Nutritional values per serving:

Total Calories: 118 kcal, **Fats:** 7 g, **Carbohydrates:** 2 g, **Protein:** 10 g

12. Cheeseburger Dumplings
Ready in: 30 mins.

Serves: 24

Difficulty: medium

Ingredients:

- 2 tbsp. of vegetable oil (30 ml)
- 1 pound of beef (454 g)
- 1/2 onion (small), minced
- 1 tbsp. of Worcestershire sauce (15 ml)

- 1 tsp. of garlic powder (5 ml)

- 1/2 tsp. of kosher salt (2.5 ml), or to taste

- 1 1/2 cups of grated cheese (170 g), Cheddar, blue cheese, Swiss, whatever you like etc.

- Black pepper, freshly grated

- 10 slices of pickles, diced (optional)

- 24 to 30 dumpling wrappers

- water for sealing wrappers

Directions:

- To prepare the filling, heat a skillet to a medium-high temperature. After adding the oil, add the onion. Cook until softened for around 1-2 minutes. Add the Worcestershire sauce, salt, black pepper, garlic powder, and ground meat. Cook the meat for 3 to 4 minutes, or until it is well cooked and browned. Take the food off the stove and let it cool.

- The cheese & optional chopped pickles should be added to the filling after the meat has cooled.

- Place around 2 tablespoons of filling in the centre of each dumpling wrapper. Spread over the edge of the wrapper after dipping your finger in the water. To seal the dumpling, gently fold it in half and press the sides together. As you close the dumpling, gently push out any extra air and flatten it.

- After beginning to roll the dumpling, wet the top edge of the wrapper to assist in sealing the end. Repeat with the remaining dumplings. Spray or brush on oil to coat.

- Arrange the dumplings in a single layer into the air fryer basket. If feasible, try to avoid having them overlap or touch.

- Air fry for 8 to 10 minutes at 182°C, flipping halfway through. Cook the wrapper until it becomes golden and crispy. In order to prevent the layers from becoming tough and chewy, if you use the bigger wrapper, cook the food for a bit longer.

- Provide warm ketchup, mustard, and barbecue sauce for dipping.

Nutritional values per serving:

Total Calories: 68 kcal, **Fats:** 4 g, **Carbohydrates:** 1 g, **Protein:** 7 g

13. Beef Tenderloin

Ready in: 47 mins.

Serves: 8

Difficulty: easy

Ingredients:

- 1 tbsp. of vegetable oil

- 2 pounds of beef tenderloin at normal temperature

- 1 tsp. of dried oregano

- ½ tsp. of cracked black pepper

- 1 tsp. of salt

Directions:

- Set the air fryer's temperature to 200°C. With paper towels, pat the beef tenderloin dry.

- The tenderloin should be put on a platter. Sprinkle oregano, salt, & pepper over the steak and drizzle the oil all over it. Incorporate oil and spices into the meat. Folding the roast to fit into the air fryer basket is necessary. Put the basket away.

- Lower the heat to 198°C. Do 22 minutes for air frying. Again turn down the heat to 182°C. Cook for a further ten minutes. The medium setting on an instant-read thermometer should read 57°C.

- The tenderloin should be taken out of the basket and placed on a platter. Before serving, let sit undisturbed for 10 minutes at least.

Nutritional values per serving:

Total Calories: 238 kcal, **Fats:** 10 g, **Carbohydrates:** 0.2 g, **Protein:** 32g

14. Steak Fajitas

Ready in: 30 mins.

Serves: 6

Difficulty: easy

Ingredients:

- 1/2 cup of diced red onion
- 2 tomatoes (large), seeded & chopped
- 1/4 cup of lime juice
- 3 tbsp. of minced cilantro (fresh)
- 1 seeded jalapeno pepper, minced
- 2 tsp. of cumin (ground), divided
- 1 beef (about 1 & 1/2 pounds) flank steak
- 3/4 tsp. of salt, divided
- 1 onion (large), halved & sliced
- Avocado slices & lime wedges optional
- 6 warmed tortillas, whole-wheat (8 inches)

Directions:

- To make salsa, combine the first five ingredients into a small dish; then, season with 1/4 tsp. Salt and 1 tsp. Cumin. Let it stand till serving.
- Set the air fryer up to 200°C. Add salt and leftover cumin to the steak. In the air-fryer basket, place it on a greased surface. Cook for 6 to 8 minutes on each side or until the meat is the desired doneness (a thermometer should, for medium-rare, register 57°C; for medium, 60°C; and for medium-well, 70°C). Take out of a basket, then stand for five minutes.
- In the meanwhile, put one onion in the air fryer basket on a tray. Cook for 2-3 minutes, stirring once, until crisp-tender. Serve steak in tortillas with salsa & onion after thinly slicing it against the grain. Serve with slices of lime and avocado, if preferred.

Nutritional values per serving:

Total Calories: 309 kcal, **Fats:** 9 g, **Carbohydrates:** 29 g, **Protein:** 27g

15. Steak Bites

Ready in: 10 mins.

Serves: 4

Difficulty: easy

Ingredients:

- 1 tbsp. of soy sauce
- ½ tbsp. of olive oil
- 16 oz. of striploin steaks in 1-inch cubes
- 1 tsp. of chilli powder
- ⅛ tsp. of salt
- ½ tsp. of black pepper
- ½ tsp. of onion powder
- ½ tsp. of garlic powder
- 1 tsp. of chilli pepper flakes
- ½ tbsp. of brown sugar

Directions:

- Set the air fryer at 200°C.
- Place the cubed steak in a mixing bowl and add the olive oil & soy sauce. Mix well till coated.
- Combine the dry ingredients in a separate small dish before adding them to the bigger bowl containing the steak cubes.
- Place the beef cubes in the basket of the air fryer and cook for 5 minutes at 200°C or till desired doneness.
- Take out of air fryer. Serve with some garlic butter on the side for dipping, garnished with chopped parsley (Optional).

Nutritional values per serving:

Total Calories: 243 kcal, **Fats:** 13 g, **Carbohydrates:** 1 g, **Protein:** 20 g

Chapter 4: Air Fried Diabetic Diet - Pork Recipes

1. Bacon Hot Dogs
Ready in: 15 mins.

Serves: 4

Difficulty: easy

Ingredients:

- 4 slices of bacon
- 4 hot dogs
- 4 buns of hot dog
- **For serving:** mustard, ketchup, BBQ sauce, jalapeños, pickles, onions, etc.

Directions:

- Tightly encircle hot dogs with strips of bacon.
- To hold the bacon securely to the hot dog, if desired, use a toothpick. Make sure the hot dogs' tips are covered with bacon. Put in the air fryer's tray or basket.
- Depending on your chosen texture, the size of the hot dogs, and how do you want your bacon, air fry for 8 to 10 minutes at 193°C. During the second half of cooking, flip the hot dogs. If you're using toothpicks, take them out before serving!
- Cook your hot dogs and bacon a bit hotter if you want them extra crispy. Follow these guidelines instead: Air fry for 6 to 8 minutes at 204°C. During the second half of cooking, flip the hot dogs. If you're using toothpicks, take them out before serving!
- Place bacon-wrapped hot dogs inside the buns & air fry for a further minute, or till the bread is warm, for warm crispy hot dog buns. Serve with your preferred garnishes.

Nutritional values per serving:

Total Calories: 321kcal, Fats: 17g, Carbohydrates: 30g, Protein: 12g

2. Bacon Zucchini Fries
Ready in: 25 mins.

Serves: 8

Difficulty: medium

Ingredients:

- 8 slices of bacon or as much as needed (in half lengthwise)
- 1 lb. (2 small to medium) of zucchini (454 g)
- oil spray
- Some black pepper
- 2 tsp. of garlic powder salt (10 ml), or to taste

Directions:

- Slice the zucchinis lengthwise, then into wedges that are 1-inch (2.5 cm) wide at the base (often quartered for small to medium-sized zucchini). Spray some oil on the zucchini lightly. Garlic powder, salt, & pepper are used to season all dishes.
- After adding bacon, add black pepper to the wrap (optional). Put the zucchini into the air fryer basket or tray after tooth-picking the bacon into it to keep it in place.
- Air Fry it at 193°C for 10 to 16 minutes, or till the bacon is as crispy as you want.
- Halfway through cooking, turn the zucchini. Prior to serving, let the food cool for a few minutes (zucchini would be very hot). Before eating, take out any toothpicks.

Nutritional values per serving:

Total Calories: 119kcal, Fats: 10g, Carbohydrates: 3g, Protein: 4g

3. Pork Belly Bites & Bbq Sauce
Ready in: 30 mins.

Serves: 4

Difficulty: medium

Ingredients:

- 1 tsp. of soy sauce or Worcestershire sauce (5 ml)
- 1 lb. of pork belly (454 g), rinsed and patted dry
- 1/2 tsp. of garlic powder (2.5 ml)
- Black pepper & salt
- 1/4 cup of BBQ sauce, sugar-free (optional)

Directions:

- Heat your Air Fryer for 4 minutes at 205°F. The pork bits will get a pretty excellent sear as a result.
- If necessary, peel the pork belly's skin. The pork belly should be cut into 3/4" cubes and put in a bowl. Worcestershire sauce, salt, garlic powder, and pepper are used to season. In the air fryer basket, distribute pork belly into a uniform layer.
- Air-fried the pork belly for 10 to 18 minutes at 205°C, shaking and rotating it twice throughout the cooking duration.
- Cook it for a further 2 to 5 minutes if you need it more done. To determine how well done the pork belly is cooked, check it.
- If preferred, season with more salt and pepper. In order to bring the tastes out, it requires a substantial quantity of spice. Add optional barbecue sauce and drizzle as desired. Serve hot.

Nutritional values per serving:

Total Calories: 590 kcal, **Fats:** 60g, **Carbohydrates:** 1g, **Protein:** 11g

---

4. Pork Egg Rolls

Ready in: 30 mins.

Serves: 12 to 14 egg role

Difficulty: medium

Ingredients:

- 2 tbsp. of vegetable oil (30 ml)
- 1 pound of ground pork (454 g)
- 3 cloves of garlic, crushed or minced
- 1 tbsp. of soy sauce (15 ml)
- 1 tsp. of ginger root, freshly grated (5 ml), optional
- 1/2 tsp. of kosher salt (2.5 ml), or to taste
- 1/2 tsp. of sesame seed oil (2.5 ml)
- Black pepper, freshly grated
- 1/2 cup of grated carrot (65 g), (about one medium carrot)
- 2 cups of cabbage (70 g), shredded thin
- 3 small green onions, chopped
- 14 egg roll wrappers (about 1 package)
- 1 egg, large
- oil spray or oil for coating the rolls

Peanut-Hoisin dip

- 1/4 cup of peanut butter (65 g)
- 1/2 cup of hoisin (140 g)
- Sriracha or hot chilli sauce (optional)
- 2 tsp. of vinegar (5 ml), or to taste
- 1/2 tsp. of sesame oil (2.5 ml), or to taste
- about half a cup of water

Directions:

- Fill each wrapper with 1-2 tbsp., of pork filling using egg roll wrappers (based on the size of the wrapper). Wrap the filling in the wrapper and tuck it inside.
- To effectively seal wrapper end, dab the top side of the wrapper with beaten egg or water. Then, continue wrapping the egg roll. Do this for each of the egg rolls. Rolls should be oiled using a brush or spray.
- Air fry for 12 to 16 minutes, turning halfway through at 195°C. Cook the wrapper until it becomes golden and crispy. In order to prevent the layers from becoming tough and chewy, if you use the bigger wrapper, cook the food for a bit longer.

- With warm peanut-hoisin dip, serve. These chicken and veggie egg rolls may also be eaten as lettuce-wrapped egg rolls!

Nutritional values per serving:

Total Calories: 152 kcal, **Fats:** 9g, **Carbohydrates:** 9g, **Protein:** 9g

5. Breaded Crispy Pork Chops
Ready in: 26 mins.

Serves: 3

Difficulty: medium

Ingredients:

- Some salt, to taste
- 3, 170g of pork chops (6oz.), rinsed and patted dry
- black pepper and smoked paprika, to taste
- Some garlic powder
- 1/2 cup of breadcrumbs (54 g), approximately
- Cooking spray to coat pork chops
- 1 egg, large

Directions:

- Season the pork chops on both sides with salt, smoked paprika, pepper, & garlic powder.
- Fill the medium bowl with the breadcrumbs. Beat the egg in a separate bowl.
- Coat each pork chop thoroughly with breadcrumbs after dipping it in the egg. Just before cooking, lightly mist the coated pork chops on both sides with cooking spray.
- For 4 minutes, preheat the air fryer up to 195°C. The pork chops will have a lovely, crispy crust as a result.
- Place in Air Fryer & cook for 8–12 minutes at 195°C. The pork chops should be cooked for a further 6 minutes after flipping them, or until browned and the internal temperature reaches 60–65°C.

- Serve hot.

Nutritional values per serving:

Total Calories: 361 kcal, **Fats:** 14g, **Carbohydrates:** 13g, **Protein:** 41g

6. Juicy Pork Chops
Ready in: 20 mins.

Serves: 3

Difficulty: medium

Ingredients:

- 2 tsp. of olive oil (10 ml) or any other preferred oil
- 3, six-ounce pork chops (170 g), rinsed and patted dry
- Some salt, to taste
- garlic powder and black pepper, to taste
- smoked paprika

Directions:

- Lightly spray or brush olive oil on the pork chops. Add smoked paprika, pepper, salt, and garlic powder for seasoning.
- Place pork chops into the Air Fryer & cook for 10–14 minutes at 194°C, turning the chops halfway through.
- Cook a bit longer if necessary to get the desired level of doneness. Serve hot.

Nutritional values per serving:

Total Calories: 287 kcal, **Fats:** 14g, **Carbohydrates:** 0g, **Protein:** 361g

7. Mushrooms Pork Bites
Ready in: 30 mins.

Serves: 4

Difficulty: medium

Ingredients:

- 8 oz. of mushrooms (227 g) (washed, cleaned and halved)
- 1 lb. of pork belly or pork chops (454 g), rinsed and patted dry
- 2 tbsp. of Butter or olive oil (30 ml), melted
- 1/2 tsp. of garlic powder (2.5 ml)
- 1 tsp. of soy sauce or Worcestershire sauce (5 ml)
- salt & black pepper, to taste

Directions:

- Heat Air Fryer for 4 minutes at 205°C. Pork will get a great sear from this.
- Combine the mushrooms and the pork chops after cutting them into 3/4" pieces (or your favourite veggie). Melt the butter or use oil, & then sprinkle garlic powder, Worcestershire sauce, salt, and pepper over the pork and mushrooms. In the air fryer basket, distribute the pork & mushrooms in a uniform layer.
- Air-fried the pork belly for 10 to 18 minutes at 205°C, shaking and rotating it twice throughout the cooking duration.
- Inspect the bits of cooked pork chop to determine how done they are. Add an additional 2 to 5 mins of cooking time if you need it more done.
- If preferred, season with more salt and pepper. Serve warm and promptly. The pork bits will become tough if they become cold.

Nutritional values per serving:

Total Calories: 241 kcal, **Fats:** 14g, **Carbohydrates:** 2g, **Protein:** 26g

8. Frozen Pork Meatballs
Ready in: 10 mins.

Serves: 3

Difficulty: easy

Ingredients:

- oil spray for coating the meatballs
- 1 lb. of Frozen Meatballs (454 g), (454g / 16 oz.)
- Tomato or BBQ Sauce, optional

Directions:

- Spread out the frozen meatballs into an equal layer in an air fryer basket (cook in batches if needed). Spray oil evenly over the meatballs.
- Gently shake and flip the meatballs midway through air-frying at 195°C for 8–12 mins. (Based on size) or till well cooked.
- Before serving, if wanted, warm your preferred sauce (tomato, BBQ, etc.) and combine it with the meatballs.

Nutritional values per serving:

Total Calories: 398 kcal, **Fats:** 32g, **Carbohydrates:** 0g, **Protein:** 26g

9. Corn Dogs
Ready in: 12 mins.

Serves: 4

Difficulty: easy

Ingredients:

- 4 Corn Dogs, Frozen (or about almost 12 oz. mini frozen corn dogs)

Directions:

- Spread out the corn dogs that are frozen into a single, uniform layer into the air fryer basket. (If your air fryer is smaller, you may have to shorten the stick a little bit to make the corn dog lie flat. The corn dogs shouldn't be tilted up near the cooking element. Oil spray is not required.
- Air fry regular-sized corn dogs for 8 minutes at 188°C. After turning the corn dogs over, cook them at 188°C for an additional 2-4 minutes, or until thoroughly cooked.
- Air fry mini-sized corn dogs for 6 minutes at 188°C. The small corn dogs should be given a little shake and turned

over, then cooked at 188°C for an additional 2-4 minutes, or till heated through.

Nutritional values per serving:

Total Calories: 190 kcal, **Fats:** 9g, **Carbohydrates:** 18g, **Protein:** 7g

---

10. Pork Roast
Ready in: 1 hr. 5 mins.

Serves: 6

Difficulty: medium

Ingredients:

- 1 tbsp. of light olive oil
- 2 lb. of pork roast
- 2 tsp. of kosher salt

Directions:

- Blot the roast pork dry. If pork roast has a rind, slice the skin in a crisscross pattern with a sharp knife. Make sure to cut into the fat under the skin rather than the meat.

- Apply salt to the skin and massage it in. Allow the salt to extract the moisture out from the skin of the pork roast by leaving it on for 10 minutes.

- Once again, pat pork roast dry, then spray more oil over it and massage it in.

- Set the air fryer oven up to 180°C.

- Cook the pork roast for 50 minutes in the air fryer basket (25 mins. per lb. of meat).

- After the allotted time has passed, check the cookedness of the pork to make sure the thickest section has achieved a temperature of 63°C.

- Ten minutes before serving, remove the pork roast from the air fryer, cover it with aluminium foil, and let it rest.

- Cut into pieces before serving

Nutritional values per serving:

Total Calories: 241 kcal, **Fats:** 35g, Carbohydrates: 0g, **Protein:** 35g

---

11. Delicious Pork Belly Fry
Ready in: 30 mins.

Serves: 1

Difficulty: Medium

Ingredients:

- 1 clove of garlic, minced
- 1 1/2 pounds of pork belly
- 1 tbsp. of fresh ginger, minced
- 2 tbsp. of rice vinegar
- 1/3 cup of hoisin sauce
- 1 tsp. of sesame oil

Directions:

- Cut the pork belly into strips that are about 3/4" and 1" broad. To fit inside the air fryer basket, cut items in half lengthwise as necessary (you'll probably need to cook in two batches).

- Put the pork belly into the air fryer and cook it there for 15 minutes at 205°C. Turn the strips to the other side and continue to air fry at 205°C for a further 7 minutes, or until golden and crisp.

- Combine the garlic, hoisin sauce, rice vinegar, ginger, and sesame oil into a small bowl and whisk to combine.

- Use a pastry brush to evenly coat the strips of pork belly in the basket of the air fryer with the sauce mixture.

- Continue to air fry for 3-4 more minutes at 205°C, or till the sauce bubbles & becomes golden.

- Take the crispy pig belly out of the basket, slice it, and serve.

Nutritional values per serving:

Total Calories: 371 kcal, **Fats:** 26g, Carbohydrates: 7g, **Protein:** 27g

---

12. Korean Pork Cheese Katsu
Ready in: 1 hr.

Serves: 8

Difficulty: medium

Ingredients:

For Pork:

- 1 lb. of pork loin (boneless), 2 oz., eight pieces
- 10 oz. of mozzarella cheese, cut into 8 or 2-inch long, 1-inch thick pieces
- salt & black pepper

For Panko:

- 3 cups of panko bread crumbs
- 3 tbsp. of avocado or any other cooking oil

Egg Mixture:

- 2 tbsp. of all-purpose flour
- 2 eggs
- 1/4 tsp. of black pepper
- 1/4 tsp. of salt

Directions:

- Sandwich a pork loin piece between two sheets of plastic or parchment paper. Pork should be flattened to a thickness of 1/8" using a heavy saucepan or meat tenderizer. Proceed with the remaining pork loin.
- Sprinkle a little salt and pepper over each pork loin piece, then top with a slice of cheese. Close the roll by rolling the side that is nearest to you, folding the right & left sides toward the centre, and rolling it shut. Pork will maintain its shape if plastic wrap is securely wrapped around it. Place for 15-30 minutes in the freezer.
- Heat a sizable skillet to a medium-high temperature. Add breadcrumbs and oil. Breadcrumbs should be toasted for 10 to 12 minutes until they are gorgeously golden brown. Frequently stir. Place aside.
- Set the air fryer to 185°C.
- Unwrap the cheese tonkatsu and dunk it in the egg mixture. Place it on the toasty breadcrumbs after evenly coating it. Spread out the bread crumbs evenly over the surface of the meat by softly pushing down. Place the cheese tonkatsu in a hot air fryer, and cook for 18-20 minutes.
- Cheese tonkatsu should be served with your preferred dipping sauce. Great sauces include steak sauce, ketchup, BBQ sauce, and tonkatsu sauce.

Nutritional values per serving:

Total Calories: 280 kcal, **Fats:** 8.6g, **Carbohydrates:** 27.2g, **Protein:** 29.4g

13. Air-fried Brats

Ready in: 15min

Serves: 5

Difficulty: easy

Ingredients:

- 1 pack of brats (uncooked)

Directions:

- Arrange the raw brats in the basket of the air fryer.
- The brats should be air-fried at 170°C for 12 to 15 minutes, turning them over halfway through. Once they achieve an inside temperature of 74°C, they are finished.
- Use tongs to take the brats out from the air fryer basket, then let them sit for five minutes to rest, then delight in them!

Nutritional values per serving:

Total Calories: 57 kcal, **Fats:** 5g, **Carbohydrates:** 2g, **Protein:** 15g

14. Pork & bok-Choy

Ready in: 1 hr.

Serves: 6

Difficulty: medium

Ingredients:

- 4 cups of bok Choy, chopped (about 12 oz.)
- 1 tbsp. of fresh ginger, chopped

- 1 tsp. of canola oil
- 1 tbsp. of garlic, chopped (3 cloves of garlic)
- 1/4 tsp. of red pepper, crushed
- 4 ounces of ground pork
- 18 wonton wrappers (3, half-inch-square) or dumpling wrappers
- Cooking spray
- 2 tsp. of soy sauce, lower-sodium
- 2 tbsp. of rice vinegar
- 1 tsp. of sesame oil, toasted
- 1 tbsp. of scallions, finely chopped
- 1 1/2 tsp. of light brown sugar, packed

Directions:

- Place a large skillet over medium to high heat and add the canola oil. Bok Choy should be added and cooked for 6 to 8 minutes, frequently turning, until mostly dry. Ginger and garlic should be added. Stir continuously for 1 minute. Place bok Choy mixture on a platter and let it cool for five minutes. With a paper towel, dry the mixture.

- In a medium bowl, combine the ground pork, bok Choy combination, and crushed red pepper.

- Lay a dumpling wrapper out on the work surface and place about 1 spoonful of filling in the middle. The edges of wrapper should be gently wetted with water using your fingertips or a pastry brush. To create a half-moon shape, fold wrapper over and press the sides together to seal. Use the leftover wrappers and filling to complete the procedure.

- Lightly spray cooking spray on the air fryer basket. Leave space between each of the six dumplings as you place them in the basket and gently mist them with cooking spray. Cook for 12 minutes at 190°C until gently browned, flipping the dumplings over halfway through. Continue in the same manner, keeping the prepared dumplings warm.

- In the meanwhile, combine the scallions, soy sauce, rice vinegar, sesame oil, and brown sugar in a small bowl and whisk until the sugar is dissolved. Put three dumplings and two tablespoons of sauce on each dish before serving.

Nutritional values per serving:

Total Calories: 140 kcal, Fats: 5g, Carbohydrates: 16g, Protein: 7g

15. Brussels Sprouts Pork Chops

Ready in: 25 mins.

Serves: 1

Difficulty: medium

Ingredients:

- Cooking spray
- 8 ounces of centre-cut, bone-in pork chop
- 1/8 tsp. of kosher salt
- 1 tsp. of olive oil
- 1/2 tsp. of black pepper, divided
- 1 tsp. of pure maple syrup
- 6 ounces of quartered Brussels sprouts
- 1 tsp. of Dijon mustard

Directions:

- Spray cooking spray lightly on the pork chop; season with salt & 1/4 tsp. of pepper. In a medium bowl, combine the remaining 1/4 teaspoon of pepper, syrup, oil, mustard, and mix in the Brussels sprouts.

- Arrange the marinated Brussels sprouts on one side of the air fryer basket and the pork chop on the other. Cook pork in air fryer at 205°C for 10–13 minutes, depending on how well-done you want your meat, or until it is golden brown and cooked through.

Nutritional values per serving:

Total Calories: 337 kcal, Fats: 11g, Carbohydrates: 21g, Protein: 40g

16. Pork Skewers with Sauce

Ready in: 35 min

Serves: 6

Difficulty: easy

Ingredients:

For skewers:

- 2 red bell peppers
- 1 lb. of pork tenderloin, fat trimmed
- ½ onion (medium)
- 2 cloves of garlic, minced or crushed
- 2 slices of bacon
- 1 tsp. of paprika
- ½ tsp. of black pepper
- ½ tsp. of salt
- 1 tbsp. of olive oil

For Creamy Maple Mustard Dipping Sauce:

- 1 tbsp. of Dijon mustard
- 2 tbsp. of mayo
- salt & pepper, to taste
- 2 tsp. of maple syrup

Directions:

- Put the diced pork into a medium bowl after cutting it into 1-inch pieces.
- Stir in the olive oil, salt, paprika, and pepper after adding the other ingredients. Place aside.
- Slice the bell peppers, onion, and bacon into 1-inch squares whilst the meat is marinating.
- Toss the chopped vegetables and bacon with the pork in the bowl to evenly distribute the marinade.
- Layer meat cubes, onions, bacon, and peppers onto metal or bamboo skewers to construct the kebabs. Use four pieces of meat on each skewer and start and finish with peppers or onions.
- Air fry for 10 to 15 minutes at 185°C, or roast for 20 to 25 minutes at 230°C

degrees, rotating once halfway through. The edges of the skewers should be thoroughly caramelized and appear golden.

- Combine the mustard, maple syrup, mayonnaise, salt, & pepper into a small bowl to create the maple mustard dipping sauce.
- If preferred, serve the pork skewers along with the dipping sauce.

Nutritional values per serving:

Total Calories: 160 kcal, **Fats:** 7.9g, **Carbohydrates:** 4g, **Protein:** 17.6g

17. Pork Loin Sandwich

Ready in: 20 min

Serves: 2

Difficulty: easy

Ingredients:

- 1/2 cup of flour
- 2 pork chops (boneless)
- 2 lightly beaten eggs
- Salt & black pepper
- 1 cup of Panko bread crumbs
- olive oil spray

Directions:

- Use the flat part of a meat tenderizer to pound 1 pork chop into a zip-top bag until it is just 1/4-inch thick.
- Gather a bowl and two plates. Fill a dish with flour. Whisk eggs, salt, and pepper in a bowl. Place bread crumbs on the final plate and season with salt and pepper.
- Take one chop that has been flattened and coat both sides with flour, then egg, and finally bread crumbs.
- Carefully put the meat in the air fryer. Spray some olive oil on.
- Air fry for five minutes at 205°C. Open the air fryer, turn, spray, & air fry for a further five minutes.

- Place on bun & top with pickles, mustard, mayo, and ketchup.

Nutritional values per serving:

Total Calories: 436 kcal, **Fats:** 15.1g, **Carbohydrates:** 39.1g, **Protein:** 35g

18. Veggie Stuffed Pork Chops

Ready in: 20 mins.

Serves: 4

Difficulty: medium

Ingredients:

- 1 chopped celery rib
- 1/2 tsp. of olive oil
- 1/4 cup of chopped onion
- 2 tbsp. of minced fresh parsley
- 4 slices of white bread, cubed
- 1/8 tsp. of salt
- 1/8 tsp. of white pepper
- 1/8 tsp. of rubbed sage
- 1/8 tsp. of dried marjoram
- 1/3 cup of chicken broth, reduced-sodium
- 1/8 tsp. of dried thyme

For chops:

- 1/4 tsp. of salt
- 4 (every 7 ounces) pork rib chops
- 1/4 tsp. of pepper

Directions:

- Heat the oil in a large skillet over medium-high heat. Cook and toss the celery and onion for 4-5 minutes, or until they are soft. Take it off the heat. Combine the bread and ingredients in a big bowl. A mixture of celery should be added together with broth.

- Slice each pork chop horizontally, nearly to the bone, to create a pocket. Add bread mixture to chops and, if necessary, secure with toothpicks.

- Set the air fryer up to 170°C. Chops should be salted and peppered. Arrange in a single layer in the air fryer basket on a greased tray. 10 minutes to cook. Turn the dish over and cook for an additional 6 to 8 minutes, or till a thermometer inserted in the stuffing's centre registers 74°C and one in the pork registers at least 74°C. After five minutes, remove toothpicks and serve.

Nutritional values per serving:

Total Calories: 10 kcal, **Fats:** 4g, **Carbohydrates:** 16g, **Protein:** 28g

Chapter 5: Air Fried Diabetic Diet ~ Poultry Recipes

1. Chicken Thighs

Ready in: 20 mins.

Serves: 4

Difficulty: easy

Ingredients:

- 1 tbsp. of olive oil
- 4 chicken thighs, bone-in (about 1 & 1/2 pounds)
- 3/4 tsp. of salt
- 1/4 tsp. of garlic powder
- 1/2 tsp. of paprika
- 1/4 tsp. of pepper

Directions:

- Set the air fryer up to 190°C. Apply oil to chicken and brush. Sprinkle the remaining ingredients over chicken after combining them. Put the chicken in the air fryer basket in one single layer on a tray with the skin-side up. Cook for 15–17 minutes, or until a thermometer placed into the chicken registers 70~75°C.

Nutritional values per serving:

Total Calories: 255kcal, Fats: 18g, Carbohydrates: 0g, Protein: 23g

2. Air fried Lemon Chicken

Ready in: 25 mins.

Serves: 4

Difficulty: medium

Ingredients:

- 3 cloves of garlic, minced
- 1/4 cup of butter, softened
- 2 tsp. of fresh rosemary, minced or 1/2 tsp. of rosemary (dried), crushed
- 1 tsp. of lemon zest, grated
- 1 tsp. of fresh thyme, minced or 1/4 tsp. of dried thyme
- 1 tbsp. of lemon juice
- 1/8 tsp. of salt
- 4 chicken thighs, bone-in (about 1 & 1/2 pounds)
- 1/8 tsp. of pepper

Directions:

- Set the air fryer up to 205°C. Combine the butter, rosemary, garlic, lemon juice, thyme, and zest in a small bowl. Each chicken thigh should have 1 tsp. of the butter mixture spread beneath the skin. Each thigh's skin should be covered with the remaining butter. Add salt and pepper to taste.
- Put the chicken in the air fryer basket with the skin-side up on a greased tray. 20 minutes of cooking, with one flip. Cook the chicken for a further 5 minutes, skin side up, or until a thermometer registers 75°–80°F.

Nutritional values per serving:

Total Calories: 329kcal, Fats: 26g, Carbohydrates: 111mg, Protein: 23g

3. Thai Air Fried Chicken Meatballs

Ready in: 10 mins.

Serves: 12

Difficulty: easy

Ingredients:

- 2 tbsp. of lime juice
- 1/2 cup of sweet chilli sauce
- 2 tbsp. of ketchup
- 1 egg (large), lightly beaten
- 1 tsp. of soy sauce
- 3/4 cup of panko bread crumbs
- 1 tbsp. of fresh cilantro, minced
- 1 finely chopped green onion
- 1/2 tsp. of salt

- 1 pound of lean ground chicken
- 1/2 tsp. of garlic powder

Directions:

- Set the air fryer up to 170°C. Combine the chilli sauce, lime juice, ketchup, and soy sauce in a small dish; save 1/2 cup for serving. Combine the egg, green onion, bread crumbs, cilantro, garlic powder, salt, and the final 4 tbsp. of the chilli sauce mixture in a sizable bowl. Add the chicken and stir just enough to combine. 12 balls should be formed.

- In the air-fryer basket, place the meatballs in batches in one single layer on a greased tray. Cook for 4-5 minutes, or until gently browned. For a further 4-5 minutes, turn the food over and cook it through until gently browned. Serve with the sauce you set out and top with more cilantro.

Nutritional values per serving:

Total Calories: 98kcal, Fats: 3g, Carbohydrates: 9g, Protein: 9g

4. Nashville Delicious Hot Chicken
Ready in: 10 mins.

Serves: 6

Difficulty: easy

Ingredients:

- 2 tbsp. of divided hot pepper sauce
- 2 tbsp. of divided dill pickle juice
- 1 tsp. of salt, divided
- 1 cup of all-purpose flour
- 2 pounds of chicken tenderloins
- 1/2 tsp. of pepper
- 1/2 cup of buttermilk
- 1 egg (large)
- Cooking spray
- 2 tbsp. of cayenne pepper
- 1/2 cup of olive oil
- 2 tbsp. of dark brown sugar

- 1 tsp. of chilli powder
- 1 tsp. of paprika
- Slices of Dill pickle
- 1/2 tsp. of garlic powder

Directions:

- Combine 1 tbsp. Pickle juice, 1 tbsp. hot sauce, and 1/2 tsp. Salt in a shallow dish or bowl. Add chicken & turn to coat. Refrigerate for at least an hour while covered. Drain the chicken, then throw away the marinade.

- Set the air fryer up to 190°C. Combine the flour, pepper, and final 1/2 tsp. of salt in a small bowl. Whisk the buttermilk, and egg with, remaining 1 tbsp. Pickle juice and 1 tbsp. Spicy sauce in a separate shallow basin. Shake off extra flour after coating the chicken on both sides. Before dipping again, coat with the egg mixture.

- Place the chicken, in batches, in one single layer on a tray that has been well oiled and placed in the air fryer basket. Cook for 5 to 6 minutes or until golden brown. Toss with cooking spray and turn. Cook for another 5 to 6 minutes or until golden brown.

- The next six ingredients should be whisked together before being poured over cooked chicken and coated. Accompany with pickles.

Nutritional values per serving:

Total Calories: 413kcal, Fats: 21g, Carbohydrates: 20g, Protein: 39g

5. Piccata Chicken Pockets
Ready in: 20 mins.

Serves: 4

Difficulty: medium

Ingredients:

- 1-1/2 cups of rotisserie chicken, shredded
- 4 sweet orange or yellow peppers (medium)
- 1-1/2 cups of brown rice, cooked

- 1/2 cup of Havarti cheese, shredded
- 1 cup of prepared pesto
- Basil leaves (Fresh), optional

Directions:

- Set the air fryer up to 205°C. Remove the seeds and stems by halving the peppers lengthwise. Peppers should be put in one single layer in the air fryer basket on a tray in batches. Cook for 10-15 minutes, or until peppers are tender and skin begins to blister. 170°C is a good temperature for the air fryer.

- In the meanwhile, mix the chicken, rice, and pesto in a big bowl. Place chicken mixture into peppers after they are cold enough to handle. Cook in batches for 5 minutes or until well heated. Add cheese and simmer for 3-5 minutes, or until it melts. Add some basil, if desired.

Nutritional values per serving:

Total Calories: 521kcal, Fats: 31g, Carbohydrates: 33g, Protein: 25g

6. Stuffed Fajita Chicken

Ready in: 15 mins.

Serves: 4

Difficulty: easy

Ingredients:

- 1 onion (small), halved & thinly sliced
- 4 skinless, boneless chicken breast, in halves (every 6 ounces)
- 1/2 green pepper (medium), thinly sliced
- 1 tbsp. of chilli powder
- 1 tbsp. of olive oil
- 1 tsp. of ground cumin
- 1/4 tsp. of garlic powder
- 1/2 tsp. of salt
- Optional: sour cream, Salsa, fresh cilantro (minced), jalapeno slices & guacamole
- 4 ounces of cheddar cheese in 4 slices

Directions:

- Set the air fryer up to 190°C. Each chicken breast's thickest region should have a pocket cut out of it horizontally. Add green pepper and onion to the space. Rub the chicken with a mixture of olive oil and spices from a small dish.

- Place the chicken in the air fryer basket in batches on a greased tray. 6 minutes to cook. Cheese pieces are added to the chicken and secured using toothpicks. Cook for another 6 to 8 minutes, or till a thermometer inserted into the chicken registers at least 74°C. Throw away toothpicks. Serve with your preferred toppings if you'd like.

Nutritional values per serving:

Total Calories: 347kcal, Fats: 17g, Carbohydrates: 5g, Protein: 42g

7. Almond Chicken

Ready in: 30 mins.

Serves: 2

Difficulty: medium

Ingredients:

- 1/4 cup of buttermilk
- 1 egg (large)
- 1 tsp. of garlic salt
- 1 cup of almonds (slivered), finely chopped
- 1/2 tsp. of pepper
- 2 skinless, boneless chicken breast, in halves (every 6 ounces)
- Optional: honey mustard or barbecue sauce, Ranch salad dressing,

Directions:

- Set the air fryer up to 170°C. Stir together the egg, buttermilk, garlic salt, and pepper in a small basin. Put almonds in a separate small dish. To help the coating stick, dip the chicken into the egg mixture and then into the almonds.

- Spread cooking spray on the greased tray where the chicken will be placed in the air fryer basket. Cook for 15–18 minutes, or until a thermometer is put into the chicken registers at least 74°C. Serve with some ranch dressing, barbeque sauce, or mustard, if preferred.

Nutritional values per serving:

Total Calories: 353kcal, Fats: 18g, Carbohydrates: 6g, Protein: 23g

8. Southern-Style Chicken
Ready in: 20 mins.

Serves: 6

Difficulty: medium

Ingredients:

- 1 tbsp. of fresh parsley, minced
- 2 cups of Ritz crackers, crushed (about 50)
- 1 tsp. of garlic salt
- 1/2 tsp. of pepper
- 1 tsp. of paprika
- 1/4 tsp. of ground cumin
- 1 egg (large), beaten
- 1/4 tsp. of rubbed sage
- Cooking spray
- 1 fryer/ broiler chicken (3-4 pounds) split up

Directions:

- Set the air fryer up to 190°C. Mix the first seven ingredients in a small dish. Put the egg in a different, small bowl. After dipping the chicken in the egg, coat it with the cracker mixture by patting it down. Chicken should be placed in single layers on a greased tray in the air fryer basket and sprayed with cooking spray in batches.

- Cook for ten minutes. Spray cooking spray after turning the chicken. Cook for 10–20 minutes more, or until the chicken is brownish and golden and the liquids are clear.

Nutritional values per serving:

Total Calories: 410kcal, Fats: 23g, Carbohydrates: 13g, Protein: 36g

9. Spicy Chicken Breasts
Ready in: 20 mins.

Serves: 8

Difficulty: medium

Ingredients:

- 2 tbsp. of Dijon mustard
- 1/2 tsp. of poultry seasoning
- 2 tsp. of salt
- 1-1/2 tsp. of garlic powder
- 2 tsp. of hot pepper sauce
- 8 (8 ounces each) chicken breast halves (bone-in), skin removed
- 1 cup of cornmeal
- 2 cups of soft bread crumbs
- 2 tbsp. of canola oil
- 1/2 tsp. of ground mustard
- 1/2 tsp. of poultry seasoning
- 1/2 tsp. of paprika
- 1/4 tsp. of dried oregano
- 1/2 tsp. of cayenne pepper
- 1/4 tsp. of parsley flakes, dried

Directions:

- Combine the first five ingredients in a big bowl. Chicken is added; turn to coat. Cover and refrigerate for an hour or overnight. The air fryer is up to 190°C.

- Drain the chicken and toss the marinade. In a small bowl, mix the remaining ingredients and whisk to blend. One piece of chicken at a time, add, & turn to coat. Place on an oiled tray in an air fryer basket in a single layer. Cook for approximately 20 minutes, rotating once halfway through or until a thermometer registers 60°C. Return all the chicken to the air fryer and heat through for an additional two to three minutes.

Nutritional values per serving:

Total Calories: 352kcal, **Fats:** 9g, **Carbohydrates:** 23g, **Protein:** 41g

10. Chicken Cordon Bleu

Ready in: 30 mins.

Serves: 4

Difficulty: medium

Ingredients:

- 1/4 tsp. of salt
- 4 skinless boneless (4 ounces each) chicken breast, in halves
- 1/4 tsp. of pepper
- 2 slices of halved Swiss cheese
- 4 slices of deli ham
- Cooking spray
- 1 cup of panko bread crumb

For sauce:

- 1/2 cup of 2% milk
- 1 tbsp. of all-purpose flour
- 1/4 cup of dry white wine
- 1/8 tsp. of salt
- 3 tbsp. of Swiss cheese, finely shredded
- Dash pepper

Directions:

- Set the air fryer up to 175°C. Chicken breasts should be salted and peppered. In the air-fryer basket, place it on a greased surface. Cook for ten minutes. Add one slice of ham and half a piece of cheese to the top of each chicken breast, covering the meat as much as you can with ham. Add some bread crumbs. Spray frying spray onto the crumbs with caution. Cook for a further 5-7 minutes or until a chicken thermometer registers 74°C.
- To make the sauce, stir together the milk and flour in a small pot. Stirring continuously, bring to a boil; simmer and

stir for one to two minutes, or until thickened.

- Lower the heat to medium. Wine and cheese should be stirred in and cooked for two to three minutes, or till cheese is melted & the sauce is bubbling and thick. Add salt and pepper and stir. Keep heated till ready to serve over low heat. Serve alongside chicken.

Nutritional values per serving:

Total Calories: 272kcal, **Fats:** 8g, **Carbohydrates:** 14g, **Protein:** 32g

11. Feta Lemon Chicken

Ready in: 25 mins.

Serves: 2

Difficulty: medium

Ingredients:

- 1-2 tbsp. of lemon juice
- 2 skinless, boneless halves of chicken breast (2 ounces each)
- 2 tbsp. of feta cheese, crumbled
- 1/4 tsp. of pepper
- 1/2 tsp. of dried oregano

Directions:

- Set the air fryer up to 205°C. Put the chicken in an air fryer-compatible baking dish that has been gently oiled. Add oregano, feta cheese, and pepper after sprinkling the chicken with lemon juice.
- Cook for 20–25 minutes, or until a thermometer registers 74°C.

Nutritional values per serving:

Total Calories: 142kcal, **Fats:** 4g, **Carbohydrates:** 1g, **Protein:** 24g

12. Chicken Parmesan

Ready in: 45 mins.

Serves: 4

Difficulty: medium

Ingredients:

- ½ cup of panko bread crumbs, plain
- ½ cup of seasoned or plain bread crumbs
- 2¼ ounces of Parmesan (½ cup), grated
- 2 eggs, large
- 2 tbsp. of Italian seasoning
- 4-8 small skinless, boneless chicken breasts (each 4-5 ounces), pounded evenly
- ¼ cup of shredded mozzarella, or to taste
- 2 tbsp. of jarred or homemade marinara sauce, and some more for serving
- Some Pasta to serve

Directions:

- To generate 4 thin chicken pieces, carefully butterfly the chicken by slicing it in half lengthwise. Sprinkle salt & black pepper on both sides of the chicken.
- Put the flour in a small bowl and season with plenty of salt and black pepper. Eggs should be blended in another shallow basin. Combine Parmesan, panko, red pepper flakes, oregano, and garlic powder in a third shallow dish.
- Coat each chicken piece in flour, brushing off any excess as you go. Finally, dip in panko mixture, gently pushing to adhere and making sure both sides of the chicken are completely coated. Dip into the eggs, letting excess drop off.
- Place chicken in an air fryer basket in a single layer, working in batches as required. Cook for five minutes on each side at 205°C, rotating once. Add mozzarella and marinara to the chicken. About 3 minutes longer of cooking time at 205°C is required for the cheese to melt and get golden.

- Arrange the chicken on each platter. Add parsley as a garnish.

Nutritional values per serving:

Total Calories: 377kcal, Fats: 13g, Carbohydrates: 32g, Protein: 37g

13. Jamaican Chicken Curry

Ready in: 30 mins.

Serves: 4

Difficulty: medium

Ingredients:

- 2 tbsp. of Jamaican curry powder
- 1 pound of skinless, boneless chicken thighs
- 2 tsp. of paprika
- 1 tsp. of adobo seasoning
- ½-1 tsp. of cayenne pepper
- ½ tsp. of salt
- 3 cloves of garlic minced
- 1 diced yellow onion
- 1 tbsp. Of olive oil

Directions:

- To a large bowl, add chicken thighs and all of the seasonings (paprika, curry powder, adobo seasoning, cayenne pepper and salt). Olive oil, minced garlic cloves, and sliced yellow onion should all be added to the bowl.
- Combine the ingredients and massage the chicken with a spoon or your hands until it is evenly seasoned on both sides. Chicken should be marinated for 30 minutes at least, but preferably several hours. Cover the bowl.
- Set the air fryer's temperature to 190°C. After the basket has heated up, coat it with frying spray, then add chicken thighs and cook for 10-15 minutes.
- When the internal temperature of the chicken reaches 74°C, flip the chicken over and cook for an additional 8 to 10 minutes.

- Dish out and savour!

Nutritional values per serving:

Total Calories: 194kcal, **Fats:** 8.6g, **Carbohydrates:** 5.89g, **Protein:** 22.84g

14. Healthy Chicken & Veggies
Ready in: 20 mins.

Serves: 4

Difficulty: medium

Ingredients:

- 1 cup of broccoli florets (frozen or fresh)
- 1 pound of chopped chicken breast, in bite-sized pieces (2 to 3 chicken breasts, medium)
- 1 chopped zucchini
- 1/2 chopped onion
- 1 cup of chopped bell pepper (any colour)
- 2 cloves of garlic, crushed or minced
- 1/2 tsp. of each garlic powder, salt, chilli powder, pepper
- 2 tbsp. of olive oil
- 1 tbsp. of Italian seasoning

Directions:

- Turn the air fryer on at 205°C.
- Slice the vegetables and chicken into bite-sized pieces, then add them to a mixing bowl.
- Toss the spice and oil together in the bowl.
- Add vegetables and chicken to the already heated air fryer, and cook for 8-10 minutes, shaking the pan halfway through, or till the chicken is well cooked. You may need to fry them in two or three batches if the air fryer is tiny.

Nutritional values per serving:

Total Calories: 230kcal, **Fats:** 10g, **Carbohydrates:** 8g, **Protein:** 26g

15. Turkey Meatballs
Ready in: 15 mins.

Serves: 5

Difficulty: easy

Ingredients:

- 1 red bell pepper, medium
- 1 & ½ lbs. of ground turkey
- ½ cup of chopped Italian parsley
- 1 tbsp. of Italian seasoning
- 1 egg, large
- ½ tsp. of black pepper, ground
- ½ tsp. of salt

Directions:

- Turn the Air Fryer's temperature up to 205°C. Get a basket of air fryers ready.
- In a bowl, combine the ground turkey, parsley, bell pepper, egg, & spices. Mix thoroughly.
- Create 1 &1/4" meatballs out of each meatball using a tablespoon or a scooper.
- Arrange the meatballs in the air fryer basket in a single layer.
- Cook for 8 to 10 minutes at 205°C, or until well cooked.
- • After the cooked meatballs have been taken out of the air fryer, cook the rest of the meatballs.

Nutritional values per serving:

Total Calories: 149kcal, **Fats:** 3g, **Carbohydrates:** 2g, **Protein:** 28g

16. Stuffed Turkey Peppers
Ready in: 30 mins.

Serves: 3

Difficulty: medium

Ingredients:

- 1 tbsp. of olive oil
- 3 red bell peppers, medium
- 12 ounces of ground turkey

- ¼ cup of panko breadcrumbs

- ½ cup of brown rice, cooked

- ¾ cup of marinara sauce, low-sodium

- ¼ tsp. of ground pepper

- 3 tbsp. of flat-leaf finely chopped parsley

- ¼ cup of shredded mozzarella cheese, part-skim (1 oz.)

- ¼ cup of Parmesan cheese, grated (1 oz.)

Directions:

- Spray cooking spray on the air fryer's basket. Pepper tops should be cut off and saved. Set aside the pepper seeds.

- In a big skillet, heat the oil over medium-high heat. Add the turkey and heat for 4 minutes, stirring periodically, until browned. Add the rice and panko and toss. Cook for approximately a minute, stirring regularly until heated through. Stir in parsley, marinara, pepper, and Parmesan after taking the pan from the heat. Among the prepared peppers, distribute the mixture equally.

- Add the peppers to the air fryer basket that has been prepared. Place the tops of pepper in the basket's base. Cook the peppers for approximately 8 minutes at 170°C or until they are soft. Add the mozzarella on top and heat for an additional 2 minutes or until the cheese is melted.

Nutritional values per serving:

Total Calories: 407kcal, Fats: 20.6g, Carbohydrates: 25.6g, Protein: 29.3g

17. Coconut Turkey Fingers

Ready in: 10 mins.

Serves: 6

Difficulty: easy

Ingredients:

- 2 tsp. of sesame oil

- 2 egg whites, large

- 1/2 cup of sweetened coconut (shredded), lightly toasted

- 2 tbsp. of sesame seeds, toasted

- 1/2 cup of bread crumbs, dry

- 1/2 tsp. of salt

- Cooking spray

- 1-1/2 pounds of turkey breast tenderloins in 1/2-inch strips

Dipping sauce:

- 1/3 cup of pineapple juice, unsweetened

- 1/2 cup of plum sauce

- 1-1/2 tsp. of prepared mustard

- Optional: lime wedges & Grated lime zest

- 1 tsp. of cornstarch

Directions:

- Set the air fryer up to 205°C. Whisk egg whites & oil together in a small bowl. Combine coconut, sesame seeds, bread crumbs, and salt in a separate shallow dish. To help the coating stick, pat the turkey after dipping it in the egg mixture and the coconut mixture.

- Working in batches, arrange the turkey in the air-fryer basket on the oiled tray in a single layer. Mist with cooking spray. Cook for 3 to 4 minutes or until golden brown. Toss with cooking spray and turn. Cook for a further 3–4 minutes or until the turkey is golden brown and no longer pink.

- Meanwhile, combine the sauce's components in a small pot. Bring to boil; simmer and stir for 1-2 minutes or until thickened. Serve sauce with the turkey. Serve turkey strips with lime wedges and, at your discretion, lime zest on top.

Nutritional values per serving:

Total Calories: 292kcal, Fats: 9g, Carbohydrates: 24g, Protein: 31g

18. Turkey Burgers

Ready in: 30 mins.

Serves: 4

Difficulty: medium

Ingredients:

- 1 egg
- 1 pound of ground turkey
- 1 tbsp. of Worcestershire sauce
- ½ tsp. of garlic powder
- 1 tsp. of salt
- ¼ tsp. of black pepper

Directions:

- All ingredients should be combined in a big bowl, then divided and formed into four patties. For five to ten minutes, or until they are solid enough to handle, freeze the turkey burger patties.
- Add the patties into the air fryer & cook for 15 minutes at 178°C, turning once.
- Add the patties in burger buns and enjoy.

Nutritional values per serving:

Total Calories: 148kcal, **Fats:** 3g, **Carbohydrates:** 1g, **Protein:** 48g

19. Turkey Fajitas

Ready in: 30 mins.

Serves: 4

Difficulty: medium

Ingredients:

- 1 tbsp. of chilli powder
- 1 tbsp. of ground cumin
- ½ tbsp. of paprika
- ½ tbsp. of dried Mexican oregano
- 1 tsp. of black pepper, freshly ground
- 1 tsp. of garlic powder
- ½ tsp. of onion powder
- 2 divided limes
- 1 pound of boneless, skinless turkey breast, in ½" thick slices
- 1 & ½ tbsp. of vegetable oil, divided
- 1 red bell pepper (large), cut into strips
- 1 yellow bell pepper (medium), cut into strips
- 1 red onion (large), halved & sliced into strips
- 1 seeded jalapeno pepper, chopped, or some more to taste
- ¼ cup of fresh cilantro, chopped

Directions:

- In a small bowl, combine the chilli powder, paprika, cumin, oregano, garlic powder, pepper, and onion powder. Over the turkey breast, squeeze the 1 lime juice. Over the meat, sprinkle the spice mixture. Include 1 tablespoon of oil. Stir to coat, then put aside.
- Add the remaining oil to the bowl with the bell peppers, onion, and salt. Coat by tossing.
- As directed by the manufacturer, heat the air fryer up to 190°C.
- In preheated air fryer, cook bell peppers & onion for 8 minutes. 5 more minutes of cooking after a shake. Put jalapenos in. For five minutes, cook. Turkey strips are added to the veggies in a single layer after the basket is opened, shaken, and then opened again. Cook for 7-8 minutes after closing the basket. Open, shake the air fryer basket to spread the mixture, and cook for an additional 5 minutes or until the peppers are soft and the turkey strips are slightly crispy & not pink anymore in the middle.
- Take the basket out, then arrange the fajitas on a dish or in a bowl. Add cilantro on top and pour the remaining lime juice over it.

Nutritional values per serving:

Total Calories: 247kcal, **Fats:** 7g, **Carbohydrates:** 15.3g, **Protein:** 32g

20. Mushroom Egg Turkey Burgers

Ready in: 50 mins.

Serves: 4

Difficulty: medium

Ingredients:

- 2 tbsp. of zucchini or mushrooms, finely grated
- 1 pound of turkey, ground (not extra lean)
- 1 egg yolk
- 1 tsp. of soy sauce
- 1 tbsp. of olive oil
- ¼ tsp. of garlic powder
- , salt & black pepper

Directions:

- In a large bowl, combine all the

  ingredients. Once combined, divide the mixture into four patties. For five to ten minutes, or until they are solid enough to handle, freeze the turkey burger patties.
- Place the patties into the air fryer & cook for 15 minutes at 178°C, turning once.
- Gently stir all the ingredients together in a bowl.
- Shape into 4 1/2-inch-thick patties. Make a tiny depression in the patties using your thumb. 30 minutes of refrigeration
- Set the air fryer up to 170°C.
- Arrange the patties into the air fryer basket in a single layer. 6 minutes to cook. Cook for a further 6 to 8 minutes on the other side or until well done (74°C).
- Top with chosen toppings and serve on buns.

Nutritional values per serving:

Total Calories: 17k6cal, **Fats:** 7g, **Carbohydrates:** 1g, **Protein:** 28g

21. Mustard Honey Turkey Breast

Ready in: 20 mins.

Serves: 5

Difficulty: medium

Ingredients:

- 2 tbsp. of olive oil
- 5 lb. of turkey (whole breast)
- 1 tsp. of salt
- 4-6 tbsp. of chopped herbs rosemary (fresh), sage, thyme
- 1 tsp. of black pepper
- 1 tbsp. of butter
- 2 tbsp. of Dijon mustard
- 3 tbsp. of honey

Directions:

- Cut the turkey along the middle to divide the 2 breasts, then preheat the air fryer up to 170°C. It should be noted that if you have a big air fryer, you might be able to cook the turkey breast in its whole.
- Rub the turkey breast with olive oil all over. Combine salt, pepper, and chopped herbs in a small bowl. Over the turkey breast, rub the herb mixture.
- Cook 1 of the halves for around 20 minutes in the air fryer. Cook the breast for 15 minutes more on the other side. Honey, Butter, and mustard are combined in a small pot over medium heat while the turkey cooks. After the butter has melted, incorporate by whisking. At this time, spread honey mustard glaze over the whole breast and put the air fryer back on for an additional 5 to 10 minutes, or until the outside is browned & crispy and the interior temperature reaches 74°C.
- Repetition is required with the other half of the turkey breast.
- Before slicing and serving, cover turkey breasts loosely with aluminium foil for 5 to 10 minutes.

Nutritional values per serving:

Total Calories: 110 kcal, Fats: 16g, Carbohydrates: 9g, Protein: 35g

22. Chicken Cutlets
Ready in: 20 mins.

Serves: 1

Difficulty: medium

Ingredients:

- ¼ cup of Parmesan cheese, grated
- 1 cup of gluten-free or whole-wheat panko breadcrumbs
- 1 tbsp. of olive oil
- ½ cup of whole buttermilk
- 1 tsp. of grated lemon zest
- 1 pound (4 cutlets) of chicken breast cutlets
- ½ tsp. of ground pepper
- ½ tsp. of salt

Directions:

- In a shallow dish, mix panko, Parmesan, oil, and lemon zest. Put the buttermilk in a different small dish.
- For five minutes, preheat the air fryer to 190°C. Spray cooking spray on the basket. Chicken should be salted and peppered. Dip in the buttermilk, allowing extra to drip off. Press the panko mixture into the surface as you dredge it. Place the basket, if required, in batches, and cook for 5 mins on each side, or till golden brown & a thermometer placed in the thickest section registers 74°C.

Nutritional values per serving:

Total Calories: 234kcal, Fats: 7g, Carbohydrates: 11g, Protein: 30g

23. Turkey Patty
Ready in: 30 mins.

Serves: 4

Difficulty: medium

Ingredients:

- 2 cloves of garlic, minced
- 1 lb. of ground turkey (454 g)
- 1 tbsp. of Worcestershire (15 ml), soy sauce or fish sauce
- 1/2 cup of minced onion (80 g)
- 1 tsp. of dried herbs (5 ml), oregano, dill, thyme, marjoram, basil
- 1/2 tsp. of salt (2.5 ml), or to taste
- Oil spray to coat
- Generous amount of Black pepper

Directions:

- For 5 minutes, preheat the air fryer to 193°C.
- Gently incorporate the turkey, dried herbs, salt, onion, pepper, Worcestershire sauce (or soy sauce or fish sauce), and garlic.
- Add ingredients for turkey patties in a bowl.
- Shape the turkey into four 4" broad patties. Apply oil evenly on both sides. You'll need to cook in 2 batches if your air fryer is smaller.
- Four patties made out of turkey flesh were coated with oil.
- Spray oil on the air fryer tray or basket or line it with a single layer of a perforated non-stick silicone liner. If necessary, cook in batches.
- Air fry for 10 to 12 minutes at 193 °C. Flip the patties after the first six minutes. Continue to Air Fry the food at 193°C for an additional 4-6 minutes, or until it reaches your ideal doneness or an internal temperature of 74°C. You may need to cook the patties for some more minutes if it is thicker. Cover the patties &

let them rest for three minutes for the juiciest results.

Nutritional values per serving:

Total Calories: 144kcal, **Fats:** 1g, **Carbohydrates:** 3g, **Protein:** 27g

24. Rotisserie Chicken

Ready in: 1 hr. 20 mins.

Serves: 6

Difficulty: medium

Ingredients:

- 1 halved lemon

- 4 sprigs of thyme, fresh

- 1 whole chicken (3 & 1/2 - 4 pound), giblets removed

- ½ tsp. of ground pepper, divided

- ¾ tsp. of salt, divided

Directions:

- Insert lemon halves and thyme sprigs into chicken cavity. Utilize kitchen twine to truss the legs of chicken shut. 3/8 tsp. Salt and 1/4 tsp. Pepper should be distributed equally throughout the breasts and legs. Put the chicken in the air fryer basket with the breasts facing up.

- No need to preheat; set your air fryer up to 170°C and cook for 25-30 minutes. Cook the chicken for 15 minutes before carefully flipping it over. Once again, carefully flip the chicken over. Cook for 10 to 15 minutes, or until a thermometer placed in the thickest part of a thigh reads 74°C. After moving the chicken to the chopping board, let it for 10 minutes to rest.

- Carve the chicken; throw away the thyme, keeping the lemon halves for later. Sprinkle the remaining 3/8 tsp. Salt and 1/4 tsp. Pepper equally over the chicken before squeezing the juice from the saved lemon halves over it.

Nutritional values per serving:

Total Calories: 166kcal, **Fats:** 6.4g, **Carbohydrates:** 1g, **Protein:** 24.8g

Chapter 6: Air Fried Diabetic Diet - Lamb Recipes

1. Lamb Chops

Ready in: 45 mins.

Serves: 4

Difficulty: medium

Ingredients:

- 2 tbsp. of red-wine vinegar
- ¼ cup of olive oil
- 1 tbsp. of fresh rosemary, chopped
- 1 tsp. of grated lemon zest
- 1 ½ tsp. of fresh oregano, chopped
- 1 clove of garlic, grated
- 1 rack of lamb (1 & 1/4-lb.), trenched, removed silver skin, & cut into single chops (about 7-8 chops)
- ¾ tsp. of black pepper, cracked
- ½ tsp. of salt

Directions:

- In a zip-top large plastic bag, combine the oil, rosemary, vinegar, oregano, garlic, lemon zest, and pepper. Place the chops in the bag after salting them. The chops should be marinated, then let stand at normal temperature for 20 minutes while being turned regularly.
- For five minutes, preheat the air fryer to 193°C. Place the chops into the basket in one single layer, and cooking spray the basket lightly (based on size of the air fryer, this might require 2 batches).
- Cook the chops for approximately 4 minutes, or until they start to brown gently. Flip, then cook for 4 to 5 minutes, or until medium-rare (34°C). (If batch cooking, remove the chops to the platter, cover, and maintain warmth. With the remaining chops, repeat.)

Nutritional values per serving:

Total Calories: 133kcal, **Fats:** 7g, **Carbohydrates:** 0g, **Protein:** 16g

2. Air Fried Lamb Roast

Ready in: 20 mins.

Serves: 2

Difficulty: medium

Ingredients:

- 1 tbsp. of olive oil
- 10 oz. or 300 g of butterflied lamb roast
- 1 tsp. of rosemary, dried or fresh
- ½ tsp. of black pepper
- 1 tsp. of thyme, dried or fresh

Directions:

- Set the air fryer to 180°C.
- On a dish, combine olive oil, rosemary, and thyme.
- After patting the lamb roast dry, throw it in the mixture of herb oil and flip it to coat it completely.
- Put the lamb in the air fryer basket and cook it for 15 to 20 minutes at 180°C.
- You should get medium-sized lamb from this. To make sure it is cooked to your preference, use a thermometer to check the temperature. If you desire it more well-done, cook it for extra 3-minute intervals.
- Take the air-fried lamb out of the fryer, wrap it in aluminium foil, and let it rest for 5 mins before serving (this will allow the juices to reabsorb in the meat).
- To serve, cut the meat against the grain.

Nutritional values per serving:

Total Calories: 181cal, **Fats:** 11g, **Carbohydrates:** 1g, **Protein:** 18g

3. Lamb Spicy Curry Puffs

Ready in: 35 mins.

Serves: 4

Difficulty: medium

Ingredients:

- 1 Egg to brush the empanadas
- 1 thawed Biscuit Dough
- 3 tbsp. of Olive Oil
- 1 tsp. of Butter, for egg wash

For Filling:

- 1 Onion (Large), thinly chopped
- 1 Cup of Lamb Mince
- 1/2 Cup of Carrots-Peas, thawed

For Spices:

- 1/4 tsp. of Ginger Powder
- 1 tbsp. of Curry Powder
- 1/8 tsp. of Garlic Powder
- Salt
- 2 tbsp. of Hot Sauce
- Black pepper

Directions:

- Set the oven temperature to 190°C.
- Add chopped onions to a pan of hot oil. Golden brown onions should be sautéed.
- Add lamb mince now, and cook for two to three mins (over medium to low flames)
- Stir in the carrot-pea mixture and cook for a further 3 to 4 minutes over medium heat, sautéing every two minutes.
- Stirring every minute, add the "Spices" to the mixture and cook for an additional 4-5 minutes.
- Remove the mixture from the heat and allow it to cool.
- Combine butter and egg in a little bowl. Split a single ball of biscuit dough into two equal pieces.

- Roll one portion into a disc and hold it in your hand. Put 2 tablespoons of the lamb filling in the centre of the circle.
- To thoroughly seal the disc, fold and pinch its edges (to make a half-moon shape).
- In a similar manner, fill the remaining dough balls. Arrange all of the lamb hand pies or lamb curry puffs onto a baking sheet.
- Evenly brush them with the egg and butter mixture.
- Bake the tray in the oven for 15 to 18 minutes or until it becomes golden brown.
- Take the puffs out of the oven and set them on a serving platter. Accompany with preferred chutney.

Nutritional values per serving:

Total Calories: 215cal, **Fats:** 14g, **Carbohydrates:** 11g, **Protein:** 11g

4. Braised Delicious Lamb-shanks

Ready in: 40 mins.

Serves: 4

Difficulty: medium

Ingredients:

- 1 & ½ tsp. of kosher salt
- 4 lamb shanks
- ½ tsp. of black pepper, freshly ground
- 2 tbsp. of olive oil
- 4 cloves of garlic, crushed
- 3 cups of beef broth, divided
- 2 tbsp. of balsamic vinegar
- 4-6 sprigs of fresh rosemary

Directions:

- Season lamb shanks with salt & pepper before setting them on the baking or drip pan. Rub the lamb all over with the minced garlic. Apply olive oil to the seasoned lamb shanks and cover with rosemary before cooking.

- Position the lamb-filled prepared pan on the rack. Choose Dual Cook. Set the temperature first to Roast for 20 minutes at 230°C & then up to Low for 2 hours at 125°C.

- Roasting the lamb requires one rotation. When the oven is set to Low, add two cups of vinegar and broth. One hour of simmering time remains; add the remaining broth.

- Lamb is cooked when the meat readily separates from the bone.

Nutritional values per serving:

Total Calories: 447cal, **Fats:** 26g, **Carbohydrates:** 6g, **Protein:** 24g

5. Air Fried Lamb & Potatoes
Ready in: 1 hr. 15 mins.

Serves: 4

Difficulty: medium

Ingredients:

- 300 g of Potatoes
- 1.2 Kg of Lamb Roast
- 1 tbsp. of Olive Oil
- 1 tsp. of thyme
- 2 tsp. of Rosemary
- Salt & Black Pepper
- 1 tsp. of Bouquet Garni

Directions:

- Score the lamb, then season it with thyme, bouquet garni, salt, and pepper.

- Put the food into the air fryer basket & set the timer for 30 minutes at 160 C.

- Place sliced and peeled roast potatoes in a bowl. Use your hands to combine the extra virgin olive oil, rosemary, salt, and pepper.

- Rotate the lamb roast and add potatoes to the spaces when the air fryer beeps. Cook at the same time & temperature for an additional 25 minutes.

- Remove the potatoes when the beeper sounds, then let the lamb rest.

- If the centre is too pink, cut it in half and continue cooking for an additional 5 mins at the normal temperature.

- Cut your lamb into slices. Enjoy after serving.

Nutritional values per serving:

Total Calories: 464kcal, **Fats:** 21g, Carbohydrates: 1g, **Protein:** 63g

6. Leg of Lamb
Ready in: 1 hr. 5 min.

Serves: 4

Difficulty: medium

Ingredients:

- Roast Potatoes
- 1.4 kg of Leg Of Lamb
- Salt & Black Pepper

Directions:

- Salt and pepper your leg of lamb then set it on the top level of the air fryer oven.

- Do 20 minutes of cooking at 180 °C. Prepare the roast potatoes as it cooks.

- When it beeps, take a little amount of the lamb juices that have fallen to the bottom of the roast potatoes, stir them, and place them on the second level.

- Cook at the same temperature for 40 minutes further before serving.

Nutritional values per serving:

Total Calories: 639.84 kcal, **Fats:** 22.55g, Carbohydrates: 319g, **Protein:** 102.78g

7. Lamb Gyro
Ready in: 45 min

Serves: 4

Difficulty: medium

Ingredients:

- 2 tbsp. of oregano
- 1 pound of ground lamb
- One tbsp. of basil
- 1/2 tbsp. of garlic powder
- 1/2 tbsp. of onion flakes or onion powders
- 1/2 tbsp. of thyme
- 1/2 tbsp. of paprika
- 1/2 tbsp. of fennel
- 1 tbsp. of Harissa Seasoning
- 1/2 tbsp. of black pepper

For Toppings:

- Romaine Lettuce
- Pita Bread
- Tomatoes
- Kalamata Olives
- Tzatziki Sauce
- Feta Cheese
- Persian Cucumbers

Directions:

- Combine the ground lamb with the harissa spices, oregano, onion flakes, basil, garlic powder, fennel, thyme, and black pepper into a small bowl. Mix thoroughly.
- Make 2-inch-wide patties out of the meat. Place for 15 to 20 minutes in the refrigerator.
- Take them out of the fridge, place your silicone liner inside, and then spray cooking spray on the liner. Set 170°C on the setting of the air fryer for 8-10 minutes. Midway during the cooking period, flip.
- Use a meat thermometer to check the internal temperature of the meat; it should be 57°C.

- Put your gyro together and serve.

Nutritional values per serving:

Total Calories: 444cal, **Fats:** 26g, **Carbohydrates:** 20g, **Protein:** 33g

8. Spaghetti & Lamb meatball muffins

Ready in: 15 min

Serves: 24

Difficulty: medium

Ingredients:

- 2 cups of Pasta Sauce
- 8.8 oz. of Pasta
- 1 slightly beaten egg
- ½ cup of Parmesan cheese, grated
- 2 cups of mozzarella cheese, shredded
- 24 cooked Lamb meatballs

Directions:

- Prepare pasta as directed on the box.
- Add 1-12 cups of marinara to the spaghetti in a big bowl. Add the beaten egg.
- To the spaghetti mixture, add 1 cup of mozzarella and 1/2 cup Parmesan, and toss thoroughly.
- Use nonstick spray to coat silicone baking ware.
- Spoon the spaghetti mixture into each cup, pushing it down firmly to make it more compact.
- Your air fryer should now include the baking cups. Ensure there is adequate space around them so that air may circulate freely. Do not crowd. Until they are completely cooked, they may be prepared in stages.
- Cook at 198°C. for 4-5 minutes. Use big tongs to remove carefully from the air fryer.
- Fill the middle of muffin cup, each with a meatball. Add some more sauce and mozzarella on top.

- Go back to the air fryer & cook for 2 more mins at 198°C.

- Use tongs to remove and place aside to cool somewhat.

- Continue making more spaghetti & meatball muffins.

- After they have cooled, you may remove them from the silicone cups & set them on a serving tray. Extra spaghetti sauce should be served on the side.

- These muffins may be frozen for later use or individually packaged for lunchboxes and snacks.

- Place in the microwave for 1 minute to warm from frozen. If it's still chilly, extend the duration by 30 seconds.

Nutritional values per serving:

Total Calories: 120kcal, **Fats:** 6g, **Carbohydrates:** 9g, **Protein:** 7g

9. Meat Filled Air Fried Pita Pockets
Ready in: 20 min

Serves: 8

Difficulty: medium

Ingredients:

- 1 onion, small

- 1 lb. of ground lamb

- 1 tsp. of salt

- ½ tsp. of allspice, ⅛ tsp. of cinnamon, ⅛ tsp. of cloves)

- 1 tsp. of sumac powder

- 1 tsp. of red pepper, crushed

- ¼ cup of olive oil

- , ½ tsp. of black pepper

- 4 (cut in half) pita bread

Directions:

- Add ground lamb or beef to a big bowl. Utilizing a food processor, grind the onion. Add onion into the bowl after draining the liquid. Mix the spices into the meat mixture after adding them.

- To let the flavours meld for a few hours at least, cover the bowl and store it in the refrigerator.

- The meat should be divided into eight equal pieces. Each pita bread should be cut in half, and the meat mixture should be gently stuffed into every pita pocket to create a layer of meat.

- Set the oven to 190°C.

- Brush the filled pitas with some olive oil on both sides, then place them onto a baking sheet. Line your baking sheet with parchment paper or foil to make cleaning simpler. Bake the pita until crispy, and the meat is heated through, about 5 mins on each side.

Nutritional values per serving:

Total Calories: 289kcal, **Fats:** 18g, **Carbohydrates:** 18g, **Protein:** 16g

10. Lamb Meatball with Tahini Sauce
Ready in: 20 min

Serves: 4

Difficulty: medium

Ingredients:

Tahini Sauce:

- Juice of two lemons

- ¾ cup of tahini paste

- 1 & ½ tsp. of kosher salt, divided

- 2–3 cloves of garlic, coarsely chopped

Meatball:

- 1 lb. of ground lamb

- 2 tbsp. of bulgur wheat, finely ground

- ½ minced yellow onion

- 1 tsp. of cumin

- 1 tsp. of coriander

- ½ tsp. of black pepper

- Oil for spraying

- ¼ tsp. of ground cinnamon

- Pita bread to serve

Directions:

- To create the tahini sauce, blitz the lemon juice, tahini paste, garlic, and 1/2 tsp. of salt in a food processor or blender until a paste forms. Slowly add 1/2 cup of cold water while the motor is running; continue blending for 1 to 2 minutes, or till sauce is smooth & pourable. Depending on the thickness of tahini paste, if the mixture still is too dense to pour, add up to an extra 1/4 cup of cold water in the same way. The sauce should be kept cold until used.

- In a heat-resistant dish, combine the bulgur with 2 tbsp., of very hot water. Stir using a fork after letting stand for seven minutes to let all the water soak.

- In a medium bowl, add the softened bulgur, lamb, onion, 1 teaspoon of salt, and spices. Mix well with your hands to make the meatballs.

- Shape the mixture of lamb into 8 equal, closely packed oval patties using wet hands to avoid sticking. The patties should be placed on a platter, covered, and chilled for 30 minutes at least and maybe overnight.

- Set the air fryer up to 205°C for 3 minutes before beginning to cook the meatballs. Spray some oil on the basket to keep the patties from clinging.

- Thread half the patties onto the metal skewers & set them into the air fryer in one single layer, working in 2 batches to prevent overcrowding the basket.

- Cook the meatball for approximately 10 minutes, flipping once halfway through or until they are browned and register 70°C on an instant-read thermometer (like this one). Continue by making the 2nd batch of patties.

- To remove any extra oil, put the fried meatball on a platter lined with paper towels. Serve with warm tahini sauce to accompany.

Nutritional values per serving:

Total Calories: 621cal, Fats: 50.7g, Carbohydrates: 17.6g, Protein: 27.2g

11. Lamb kebab
Ready in: 20 min

Serves: 4

Difficulty: medium

Ingredients:

- 1 pound of ground lamb (480 g)
- 1 tbsp. of cooking oil
- 1/4 cup of fresh parsley, chopped
- 2 tbsp. of kebab spice mix
- 1 tbsp. of minced garlic
- 1 tsp. of kosher salt

Directions:

- All ingredients should be combined in a big mixing dish. Blend with an immersion blender until uniform. Refrigerate the lamb mixture for 30 minutes, at least with a cover on.

- For five minutes, preheat the air fryer up to 200 C.

- Take the chilled lamb mixture out of the fridge. The mixture should be shaped into four long sausages using your hands. Enter bamboo skewers that have been socked.

- Kebabs should be put in the basket of an air fryer. Fry for 8-10 minutes or till internal temperature reaches 70°C with tzatziki sauce, and serve.

Nutritional values per serving:

Total Calories: 140.9cal, Fats: 8.4g, Carbohydrates: 1.3g, Protein: 9.4g

12. Lamb & Cauliflower Rice
Ready in: 25 mins.

Serves: 2

Difficulty: medium

Ingredients:

- 1/3 cup of Frozen Corn (46g)

- 12 oz. bag of Cauliflower Rice, Frozen
- 1/3 cup of Peas & Carrots, Frozen (42g)
- 1 tbsp. of Soy Sauce (15g)
- 1 tbsp. of toasted Sesame Oil (16g)

Optional:

- 1/2 tsp. of Ginger, Ground
- 1/2 tsp. of Garlic Powder

Directions:

- Put the cauliflower rice into a dish that can be used in an air fryer or covers the bottom of basket with foil. 10 minutes of air frying at 205°C.
- Sesame oil & soy sauce should be added to the rice. Before adding the ginger & garlic powder and the other vegetables, give the rice a quick stir to coat it.
- Air-fried the rice for a further 10 to 15 minutes at 205°C while tossing regularly or until it reaches your desired crispiness. Add green onions as a garnish and season with some salt and pepper.

Nutritional values per serving:

Total Calories: 155cal, Fats: 7g, Carbohydrates: 15g, Protein: 7g

13. Butter Potato Lamb Chops

Ready in: 17 min

Serves: 1

Difficulty: easy

Ingredients:

- Salt & black pepper
- 350 g of lamb chops
- 1 tbsp. of butter
- 2 potatoes (large)
- 3-4 stalks of rosemary herbs

Directions:

- Rub salt, pepper, & rosemary herbs all over lamb chops to make a marinade.
- Peel and chop the potatoes into tiny pieces. Combine the butter, salt, and

pepper with the rosemary sprigs that have been crushed.

- Heat up the air fryer.
- Put the ingredients in the air fryer and cook for 10 minutes at 200°C. To make sure food is cooked evenly when air frying, shake and turn the contents halfway through.
- Enjoy!

Nutritional values per serving:

Total Calories: 380kcal, Fats: 20g, Carbohydrates: 34g, Protein: 28g

14. Stuffed Lamb Feta Burgers

Ready in: 50 mins.

Serves: 5

Difficulty: medium

Ingredients:

For burger patties:

- 1 lb. of ground lamb
- 8 oz. of mushrooms
- ¼ tsp. of salt
- 4 oz. of crumbled feta
- ¼ tsp. of pepper

For pickled red onions:

- ½ cup of water
- 1 sliced thinly red onion
- ½ cup of distilled white vinegar
- 1 tsp. of salt
- 2 tbsp. of honey

For yoghurt sauce:

- 1 tbsp. of lemon juice
- ½ cup of plain Greek yoghurt, nonfat
- ½ tbsp. of olive oil
- ¼ tsp. of garlic powder
- ¼ tsp. of salt

- 1 tbsp. of fresh parsley
- 1 tbsp. of fresh dill

For assembling burger:

- ¾ cup of baby arugula
- 5 hamburger buns

Directions:

- Make the hamburger patties first. The mushrooms should first be roughly chopped and added to the food processor. Several pulses are needed to achieve extremely fine chopping.

- Combine the minced mushrooms, salt, ground lamb, and pepper in a big bowl. Mix well using your hands. Divide into ten equal pieces.

- Make a patty by taking one piece of lamb mixture. In the middle, sprinkle some feta. Place another patty made from leftover lamb mixture on top, sealing the sides by squeezing them together. To create 5 filled burger patties, repeat the process with the leftover lamb mixture and feta.

- The patties should be placed on a platter and chilled in the refrigerator for 20 minutes at least.

- If you want to make pickled red onions from scratch, get started on them in the meanwhile. In a mason jar, put your finely sliced onion. Combine the vinegar, water, honey, & salt in a small saucepan. After bringing it to a boil, turn off the heat. After covering the onions with the vinegar mixture, wait 10 minutes.

- Additionally, make the yoghurt sauce. Greek yoghurt, olive oil, lemon juice, salt, dill, garlic powder, and parsley should all be mixed together in a bowl. Combine and put away for the time being.

- When the patties are cool enough to handle, take them from the burgers and put them in the air fryer's basket. Work in batches if necessary.

- Air-fried the lamb patties at 190°C for 15 to 18 minutes, or until they reach an inside temperature of 70°C.

- The Greek yoghurt sauce, arugula, a dollop of the pickled red onions, & the lamb patties should be placed on a bun. Enjoy!

Nutritional values per serving:

Total Calories: 480kcal, **Fats:** 11.5g, **Carbohydrates:** 1.5g, **Protein:** 32g

Chapter 7: Air Fried Diabetic Diet ~ Fish & other Seafood Recipes

1. Breaded Sea Scallops

Ready in: 15 mins.

Serves: 4

Difficulty: easy

Ingredients:

- ½ tsp. of garlic powder
- ½ cup of buttery crackers, finely crushed
- ½ tsp. of seafood seasoning
- 1 pound of sea scallops (dry)
- 2 tbsp. of butter, melted
- 1 cooking spray

Directions:

- Set the air fryer's temperature to 198°C.
- In a small bowl, combine the garlic powder, cracker crumbs, and seafood seasoning. Put butter in a 2nd shallow dish after it has melted.
- Roll each scallop in breading till thoroughly covered, then dip in the melted butter. Repeat with remaining scallops, then place on a dish.
- Lightly spritz cooking spray in the air fryer basket. You may have to work in batches. Arrange the scallops into the prepped basket so that they're not overlapping.
- Do 2 minutes of cooking in the already heated air fryer. With a tiny spatula, carefully flip the scallops over and cook for an additional 2 minutes or until opaque.

Nutritional values per serving:

Total Calories: 282kcal, Fats: 17.6g, Carbohydrates: 13.7g, Protein: 16.6g

2. Crumbed Fish

Ready in: 25 mins.

Serves: 4

Difficulty: medium

Ingredients:

- 4 flounder fillets
- ¼ cup of vegetable oil
- 1 sliced lemon
- 1 beaten egg

Directions:

- Set an air fryer up to 180°C.
- Combine oil and bread crumbs in a small bowl; whisk until the mixture is loose and crumbly.
- Shake off any extra egg after dipping fish fillets in it. Dip the fillets into the bread crumbs mixture and completely coat them.
- Gently place the coated fillets into the air fryer basket and heat for 12 minutes, or until the fish with a fork easily flakes. Serve with lemon slices as a garnish.

Nutritional values per serving:

Total Calories: 353kcal, Fats: 17.7g, Carbohydrates: 22.5g, Protein: 26.9g

3. Salmon Cakes & Sriracha Mayo

Ready in: 40 mins.

Serves: 4

Difficulty: medium

Ingredients:

Sriracha Mayo:

- 1 tbsp. of Sriracha
- ¼ cup of mayonnaise

Salmon Cakes:

- ⅓ cup of almond flour
- 1 pound of salmon fillets (skinless), cut into 1-inch pieces
- 1 lightly beaten egg

- 1 coarsely chopped green onion
- 1 ½ tsp. of seafood seasoning
- 1 pinch of seafood seasoning
- cooking spray

Directions:

- In a small bowl, combine Sriracha and mayonnaise. Put 1 tablespoon of the Sriracha mayo into the food processor's bowl, then chill the remaining mixture until needed.

- To the Sriracha mayo, add the salmon, egg, almond flour, 1 1/2 tsp. of seafood spice, and green onion. Pulse briskly for 4-5 seconds, just until the ingredients are incorporated, but there are still tiny pieces of salmon visible. (Avoid over-processing as it will make the mixture mushy.)

- Spread cooking spray on hands and cover a dish with waxed paper. Make 8 little patties out of the salmon mixture, then place them on a platter. Place in the fridge for 15 minutes or until cooled and stiff.

- Set the air fryer's temperature to 200°C. Spray cooking oil on the air fryer basket.

- Take the salmon cakes out of the fridge. Working in the batches, if required to prevent crowding, lightly coat both sides with the cooking spray before placing it into the air fryer basket.

- Cook for 6-8 minutes in the already heated air fryer. Place on a serving tray and serve with any leftover Sriracha mayo and, if preferred, a small dusting of Old Bay seasoning.

Nutritional values per serving:

Total Calories: 340kcal, Fats: 24.7g, Carbohydrates: 3.6g, Protein: 25.5g

4. Lemon Pepper Shrimp
Ready in: 15 mins.

Serves: 2

Difficulty: medium

Ingredients:

- 1 juiced lemon
- 1 tbsp. of olive oil
- 1 tsp. of lemon pepper
- ¼ tsp. of garlic powder
- ¼ tsp. of paprika
- 1 sliced lemon
- 12 ounces of medium shrimp (uncooked), peeled & deveined

Directions:

- Set an air fryer to the manufacturer's recommended temperature of 200°C.

- Oil, lemon pepper, lemon juice, paprika, & garlic powder should all be combined in a bowl. Add the shrimp and coat well.

- Cook shrimp into the preheated air fryer for 6 to 8 minutes, or until the outsides are brilliant pink and the interiors are opaque. Add lemon wedges to the dish.

Nutritional values per serving:

Total Calories: 215kcal, Fats: 8.6 g, Carbohydrates: 12.6g, Protein: 28.9g

5. Lobster Tails with Garlic-Lemon Butter
Ready in: 20 mins.

Serves: 2

Difficulty: medium

Ingredients:

- 4 tbsp. of butter
- 2 lobster tails (4 ounces)
- 1 tsp. of lemon zest
- salt & black pepper (ground), to taste
- 1 clove of garlic, grated
- 2 lemon wedges
- 1 tsp. of fresh parsley, chopped

Directions:

- Set an air fryer up to 195°C.

- Use kitchen shears to cut longitudinally through the centres of the flesh and hard top shells of lobster tails. Cut up to the bases of the shells but not beyond them. Disperse the tail parts. Place the lobster meat-facing-up on the tails in air fryer basket.

- In a saucepan set over medium heat, melt the butter. Add garlic and lemon zest; cook for 30 seconds or until garlic is aromatic.

- Spoon 2 tablespoons of the butter mixture into a small dish, then brush it over the lobster tails. Discard any excess butter to prevent cross-contamination with the raw lobster. Use salt and pepper to season lobster.

- Cook in the already heated air fryer for 5 to 7 minutes, or until the lobster flesh is opaque.

- Pour the saucepan's saved butter over the lobster flesh. Serve with lemon wedges and parsley on top.

Nutritional values per serving:

Total Calories: 313kcal, **Fats:** 25.8g, **Carbohydrates:** 3.3g, **Protein:** 18.1g

6. Salmon Nuggets
Ready in: 35 min

Serves: 4

Difficulty: hard

Ingredients:

- ¼ tsp. of dried chipotle pepper, ground

- ⅓ cup of maple syrup

- 1 pinch of sea salt

- 1 egg (large)

- 1 ½ cups of garlic-flavoured croutons & butter

- cooking spray

- 1 centre-cut, skinless salmon fillet (1 pound), cut in 1 & 1/2-inch of chunks

Directions:

- In a saucepan, combine salt, maple syrup, and chipotle powder. Heat to a simmer. To stay warm, turn the heat down to low.

- In the bowl of the small food processor, add the croutons and pulse several times to create fine crumbs. Place in a small bowl.

- Set the air fryer up to 198°C and whisk the egg in a different bowl.

- Lightly season salmon with sea salt. Salmon should be lightly dipped into the egg mixture, allowing excess drop-off. Shake off any excess crouton breading after coating the fish. Put onto a plate and give a gentle cooking spray mist.

- Cooking spray should be used on the air fryer's basket. If necessary, add salmon nuggets within, working in the batches to prevent crowding.

- Do 3 minutes of cooking in a preheated air fryer. Turn the salmon pieces gently, spritz with a little oil, and cook for an additional 3 to 4 minutes, or until the fish is well cooked. Drizzle heated chipotle maple syrup over the dish before serving. Serve right away.

Nutritional values per serving:

Total Calories: 364cal, **Fats:** 16.4g, **Carbohydrates:** 27.2g, **Protein:** 25.8g

7. Fish Sticks
Ready in: 20 mins.

Serves: 4

Difficulty: easy

Ingredients:

- ¼ cup of all-purpose flour

- 1 pound of cod fillets

- 1 egg

- ¼ cup of grated Parmesan cheese

- ½ cup of panko bread crumbs

- 1 tbsp. of parsley flakes

- ½ tsp. of black pepper

- 1 tsp. of paprika
- cooking spray

Directions:

- Set an air fryer up to 200°C.
- Cut fish into 1x3-inch sticks after patting it dry with paper towels.
- Fill a shallow plate with flour. In a separate, shallow dish, beat the egg. In a 3rd shallow dish, mix panko, parsley, Parmesan cheese, paprika, & pepper.
- Use flour to cover each fish stick before dipping it in a beaten egg and then coating it with a seasoned panko mixture.
- Coat the air fryer's basket with nonstick frying spray. Make sure none of the sticks contacts you when you arrange half of them in the basket. Each stick's top should be sprayed with cooking spray.
- Five minutes of cooking in the already heated air fryer. Cook the fish sticks on the other side for five more minutes. With the remaining fish sticks, repeat.

Nutritional values per serving:

Total Calories: 200kcal, Fats: 4.1g, Carbohydrates: 16.5g, Protein: 26.3g

8. Panko-Crusted Mahi Mahi

Ready in: 20 mins.

Serves: 4

Difficulty: medium

Ingredients:

- 2 tbsp. of Grapeseed oil
- 4 Mahi Mahi fillets (4 ounces)
- 2 cups of panko bread crumbs
- ½ tsp. of garlic salt
- 1 tsp. of everything bagel seasoning
- ½ tsp. of ground turmeric
- Cooking spray
- ½ tsp. of ground black pepper
- 1 lemon (medium), cut in 4 wedges

- 1 tsp. of fresh parsley, chopped

Directions:

- For five minutes, preheat the air fryer up to 200°C.
- Mahi Mahi fillets should be placed on a tray and covered with Grapeseed oil in the meanwhile.
- In a shallow dish, combine panko, garlic salt, bagel seasoning, turmeric, & pepper. Place the fillets in the basket of the air fryer in one single layer after coating each with the panko mixture. Use nonstick spray to coat.
- Cook in the already heated air fryer for 12 15 minutes, turning halfway through, or till fish easily flakes with a fork.
- Take out of the air fryer. Lemon wedges and parsley are used as a garnish. Serve right away.

Nutritional values per serving:

Total Calories: 304kcal, Fats: 9.4g, Carbohydrates: 40.6g, Protein: 26.7g

9. Spicy Bay Scallops

Ready in: 15 mins.

Serves: 4

Difficulty: easy

Ingredients:

- 2 tsp. of smoked paprika
- 1 pound of bay scallops, rinsed & patted dry
- 2 tsp. of chilli powder
- 1 tsp. of garlic powder
- 2 tsp. of olive oil
- ⅛ tsp. of red cayenne pepper
- ¼ tsp. of ground black pepper

Directions:

- Set an air fryer up to 200°C.
- Stir the following ingredients in a bowl: bay scallops, chilli powder, smoked paprika, garlic powder, olive oil, pepper,

& cayenne pepper. Transfer to the basket of an air fryer.

- Shake the basket halfway through air-frying the scallops for 8 minutes, or until they are well done.

Nutritional values per serving:

Total Calories: 179kcal, **Fats:** 3.8g, **Carbohydrates:** 7.2g, **Protein:** 28.9g

10. Crunchy Seasoned Cod Fillets
Ready in: 22 mins.

Serves: 3

Difficulty: medium

Ingredients:

- ⅓ cup of panko bread crumbs, unseasoned
- Cooking spray (avocado oil)
- ⅓ cup of yellow cornmeal, stone-ground
- 1 tsp. of paprika
- 2 tsp. of seasoning mix
- ½ tsp. of salt
- 3 cod fillets (5 ounces)
- ½ cup of buttermilk
- 1 tbsp. of all-purpose flour

Directions:

- In the base of the basket of the air fryer, make a 3-inch wide foil sling that extends across the bottom & up the sides. Make some holes in the foil sling's bottom that correspond to the holes in the basket. Use avocado oil to spritz on the sling.
- Set the air fryer's temperature to 200°C.
- In a separate bowl, mix the panko crumbs, seasoning mix, yellow cornmeal, paprika, and salt. Add buttermilk to a different bowl.
- After gently dusting both sides of the cod fillets with flour, pat them dry with paper towels. Each flour-coated fillet should be dipped into buttermilk before being coated with the crumb mixture. Place each fillet on a foil sling, if you're using it,

or onto the rack of the shelf-style air fryer, and pat all sides with the crumb mixture. Spray avocado oil on each fish fillet.

- Cook in the air fryer for 10 to 12 minutes, or till the fish flakes easily. Cod fillets should be taken out of the air fryer using the sling and served right away.

Nutritional values per serving:

Total Calories: 224kcal, **Fats:** 2.3g, **Carbohydrates:** 23.1g, **Protein:** 29.5g

11. Salmon Patties
Ready in: 25 mins.

Serves: 6

Difficulty: easy

Ingredients:

- 1 tbsp. of brown sugar
- 2 tbsp. of grill seasoning
- ¾ tsp. of ground cumin
- ¼ tsp. of cayenne pepper
- ½ tsp. of ground coriander
- 2 pounds of skin on salmon fillets

Directions:

- For 2 minutes, preheat the air fryer to the 165°C setting for fish.
- In a small bowl, mix the cayenne pepper, cumin, brown sugar, coriander, & steak seasoning. Each salmon fillet should receive around 2 tsp. (or more, as preferred) of the seasoning mixture. Salmon should be layered into the air fryer basket.
- Cook salmon into the air fryer for approximately 18 minutes, or until it easily flakes with a fork, working in batches if required. Place cooked salmon on a platter and rewarm on the lowest setting of the oven. The remaining salmon fillets, and repeat. Serve right away.

Nutritional values per serving:

Total Calories: 230kcal, **Fats:** 9.8g, Carbohydrates: 3.5g, **Protein:** 30.2g

12. Lemon-Garlic Salmon
Ready in: 25 mins.

Serves: 2

Difficulty: medium

Ingredients:

- ½ tsp. of minced garlic
- 1 tbsp. of melted butter
- 2 fillets of salmon fillets, centre-cut (6 ounces), with skin
- ⅛ tsp. of dried parsley
- ¼ tsp. of lemon-pepper seasoning
- 3 thin slices of lemon in half
- cooking spray

Directions:

- Set the air fryer's temperature to 200°C.
- Melted butter & minced garlic are combined in a small bowl.
- Salmon fillets should be rinsed and dried with paper towels. Brush with the butter mixture and garnish with parsley and lemon-pepper seasoning.
- Cooking spray should be used on the air fryer's basket. Put three lemon halves on top of each salmon fillet into the basket, skin side down.
- Cook for 8-10 minutes in the already heated air fryer. Take out of the air fryer, then wait two minutes before serving.

Nutritional values per serving:

Total Calories: 293kcal, **Fats:** 16.4g, Carbohydrates: 1.4g, **Protein:** 33.6g

13. Crispy Parmesan Cod
Ready in: 25 mins.

Serves: 4

Difficulty: medium

Ingredients:

- salt and black pepper
- 1 pound of cod filets
- 1/2 cup of flour
- 1/2 tsp. of salt
- 2 eggs (large)
- 1 cup of Panko
- 2 tsp. of old bay seasoning
- 1/2 cup of grated parmesan
- olive oil spray
- 1/2 tsp. of garlic powder

Directions:

- Cod fillets should be salted and peppered.
- Establish a station for breading fish. Add the flour to a bowl. The eggs and salt should be combined in the second bowl. Add the Panko, old bay seasoning, parmesan cheese, and garlic powder to the final bowl.
- Cod should first be floured.
- Next, add the egg concoction.
- In the Panko, finally.
- Apply olive oil with a spray bottle to the basket's bottom. Put the fish into the air fryer's basket. Cook for 10 minutes at 205°C. Flip the fish gently. Cook the meat for a further 3–5 minutes, or until it reaches a temperature of 57°C, inside.

Nutritional values per serving:

Total Calories: 303 kcal, **Fats:** 3 g, Carbohydrates: 24g, **Protein:** 32g

14. Chili Lime Tilapia
Ready in: 10 mins.

Serves: 2

Difficulty: easy

Ingredients:

- 2 tsp. of chilli powder
- 12 oz. of tilapia fillets, 6 to 8 oz. each
- 1 tsp. of cumin

- 1/2 tsp. of oregano
- 1 tsp. of garlic powder
- 1/2 tsp. of sea salt
- 1 Lime zest
- 1/4 tsp. of ground black pepper
- Juice of half lime

Directions:

- If the air fryer has to be heated up, do it at 205°C. Use your preferred cooking oil to coat the air fryer tray or basket.
- Use a paper towel to pat the tilapia fillets dry.
- Place all the spices in a small bowl, except the lime juice, and mix to blend.
- Apply the spice mixture evenly over the fish.
- Cook fish into the air fryer, apart from one another, for 8 to 10 minutes, or until opaque and flaky.
- Serve right after adding lime juice.

Nutritional values per serving:

Total Calories: 178kcal, Fats: 3g, Carbohydrates: 3g, Protein: 35g

15. White Fish with Lemon Pepper and Garlic

Ready in: 16 mins.

Serves: 2

Difficulty: easy

Ingredients:

- 2 tbsp. of olive oil
- 4 white fish filets (6 oz.)
- 2 tsp. of garlic powder
- 1 tsp. of freshly cracked pepper
- 1 tsp. of Celtic sea salt
- 1 sliced lemon, in thin rounds
- 2 tsp. of Italian herbs
- 1 tsp. of lemon juice

Directions:

- Place the fish fillets in a big bowl, add the lemon juice and olive oil, and toss to coat the fish evenly.
- Season liberally with Italian herbs, salt, and pepper.
- Arrange the fish fillets in the air fryer basket so that they don't contact one another excessively.
- Fish should be placed in an air fryer basket with lemon slices all around it.
- For fish with a slight bit of red in the centre, preheat the air fryer up to 205°C & cook for 10 minutes.
- For fish without any red in the centre, cook for 12 minutes; for well-done or fatter fish fillets, cook for 14.
- Dish out and savour!

Nutritional values per serving:

Total Calories: 462kcal, Fats: 28g, Carbohydrates: 13g, Protein: 39g

16. Crispy Fish Tacos & Pineapple Slaw

Ready in: 35 mins.

Serves: 4

Difficulty: easy

Ingredients:

- 1 & 1/4 tsp. of garlic powder
- 1 cup of panko bread crumbs
- 1 & 1/2 tsp. of chilli powder
- 1 tsp. of ground cumin
- 1/2 tsp. of onion powder
- 3/4 tsp. of kosher salt
- 24 oz. of barramundi (4 filets)
- 1/4 tsp. of black pepper
- 1 egg, large, plus 2 tbsp. of water
- sour cream & lime juice, to serve
- 16 flour tortillas

Salsa:

- 2 tsp. of honey
- 2 tbsp. of lime juice
- 1 clove of garlic (small), grated
- 1/2 tsp. of ground cumin
- 1/2 tsp. of kosher salt
- 1/2 tsp. of chilli powder
- 5 cups of shredded cabbage
- 2 tbsp. of olive oil
- 1 jalapeno, diced
- 1/4 cup of chopped cilantro
- 1 cup of chopped pineapple
- 1/4 cup of red onion, diced

Directions:

- Set the fryer's temperature to 195°C for five minutes.

- Combine the panko, salt, cumin, black pepper, chilli powder, garlic powder, onion powder, and chilli powder in a shallow plate or bowl. To blend, stir.

- In a bowl or shallow dish, combine the egg and water. Combine by whisking.

- Use paper towels to pat dry the fish. Cut fish into 4, 1x4 pieces using a sharp knife. Add salt and pepper to taste.

- Submerge every piece of the fish in the egg. Allow the extra to trickle off. Add the bread crumbs to coat. Ensure the breadcrumbs are pushed into the fish using your fingers. Continue with the remaining fish.

- Fill the air fryer with half the fish. Use a lot of olive oil spritz on the top. For 4 minutes, cook. Flip over the fish by removing the tray. Use olive oil spray to spritz. Cook for a further 2 minutes or until crispy and golden. After every batch, clean the air fryer's bottom. It is really fast and simple & prevents fish from burning later. Repeat with the second fish, half of it.

- While the fish is cooking, in a medium bowl, combine the honey, lime juice, garlic, cumin, salt, chilli powder, and olive oil. Combine by whisking. Add the cilantro, red onion, pineapple, cabbage, and jalapenos. Toss to evenly distribute the dressing. Use salt and pepper to taste to season.

- Microwave tortillas to a warm state. Over an open heat, you may burn the tortillas if you want.

- Fill each tortilla with a little amount of slaw. Add a slice of fish on top. Add additional coleslaw on top. Serve with some lime juice & sour cream.

Nutritional values per serving:

Total Calories: 82kcal, Fats: 3g, Carbohydrates: 5g, Protein: 9g

---

17. Swordfish Steak & Mango Citrus Salsa

Ready in: 15 mins.

Serves: 1

Difficulty: easy

Ingredients:

- 1/2 mango
- 1 swordfish steak
- half jalapeno
- 1 tbsp. of orange juice
- 1/4 onion
- juice of half lime
- salt and black pepper, to taste
- Some cilantro

Directions:

- Swordfish should be salted and peppered. Cook for 8 to 10 mins at 205°C in the air fryer. No flipping is required.

- Make a medium bowl of chopped mango, onion, jalapeño, and cilantro for the citrus salsa. Juices from the orange and lime may be added; mix.

- Remove the fish from the air fryer with care, place it on a dish, and cover it with salsa. Enjoy!

Nutritional values per serving:

Total Calories: 442kcal, **Fats:** 9g, **Carbohydrates:** 65g, **Protein:** 27g

18. Crab Cakes
Ready in: 40 mins.

Serves: 6

Difficulty: medium

Ingredients:

- 2 tbsp. of butter (unsalted), melted
- 2 eggs (large)
- 1 tbsp. of fresh basil, chopped
- 2 tsp. of Worcestershire sauce, lower-sodium
- 2 tsp. of fresh tarragon, chopped
- 1 tsp. of lemon zest (grated), plus some lemon wedges, to serve
- ½ tsp. of garlic powder
- 1 tsp. of Old Bay seasoning, reduced-sodium
- ½ tsp. of onion powder
- 2 tbsp. of fresh chives (thinly sliced), divided
- ½ cup of sour cream (light), divided
- 1 pound of lump crabmeat (fresh) or 3 cans of lump crab meat (6 ounces), drained & picked over
- Cooking spray
- ½ cup of panko breadcrumbs, whole-wheat
- 6 butter lettuce leaves (large)

Directions:

- Set a 6 & 1/2-quart air fryer up to 195°C before using. In a large bowl, combine eggs, butter, chives, tarragon, basil, Worcestershire, lemon zest, garlic powder, Old Bay, onion powder, and 1/3 cup sour cream. Gently toss in the panko and crab meat.
- Using clean hands, form the mixture into six crab cakes, each measuring 1/3 cup. Spray frying oil on the fry basket liberally.

3 crab cakes should be added, each of which should be covered with frying spray. Cook for 15 to 18 minutes, rotating once and spraying halfway with extra frying spray, until well browned & crispy on both sides. Place on a platter and cover to maintain warmth. Continue by making the rest of 3 crab cakes.

- Arrange one lettuce leaf and one crab cake on each of the six dishes. 1 & 1/2 tsp. of sour cream & 1/2 tsp. of chives should be placed on top of each crab cake. If desired, garnish with lemon slices. Remove the fish from the air fryer with care, place it on a platter, and cover it with salsa. Enjoy!

Nutritional values per serving:

Total Calories: 209kcal, **Fats:** 4g, **Carbohydrates:** 7g, **Protein:** 22g

19. Bacon Wrapped Shrimp
Ready in: 30 mins.

Serves: 8

Difficulty: medium

Ingredients:

- 8 slices of bacon in thirds
- 24 tail on jumbo shrimps (raw), deveined, thawed from frozen or fresh
- 1 tbsp. of olive oil
- 1 ~2 cloves of garlic, minced
- 1 tsp. of paprika
- 1 tbsp. of fresh parsley, finely chopped

Directions:

- Combine olive oil, garlic, paprika, and parsley in a small bowl.
- If necessary, peel the tails off of the raw shrimp and set them in a medium dish.
- Drizzle the shrimp with the olive oil mixture and gently swirl to coat.
- Place each shrimp on a small baking sheet and wrap a bacon strip around the centre, seam side down.

- Chill for 30 minutes. (Bacon is kept in place during cooking, thanks to this.)

- Set the air fryer at 205°C.

- Place the shrimp seam-side down, snugging the bacon again if required. Take care to avoid having the shrimp overlapping or touching. (Depending on the size of the air fryer, cooking may need to be done in batches.)

- Cook the bacon for 8-10 minutes or until it is completely done. If required, repeat with the remaining shrimp. Serve right away.

Nutritional values per serving:

Total Calories: 111kcal, **Fats:** 11g, **Carbohydrates:** 1g, **Protein:** 3g

20. Shrimp Scampi

Ready in: 15 mins.

Serves: 4

Difficulty: medium

Ingredients:

- 1 tbsp. of Lemon Juice

- 4 tbsp. of Butter

- 1 tbsp. of Garlic, Minced

- 1 tbsp. of chives (chopped), or 1 tsp. of dried chives

- 2 tsp. of Red Pepper Flakes

- 1 tbsp. of fresh basil (chopped), or 1 tsp. of dried basil

- 1 lb. of Raw Shrimp (453.59 g), (21 to 25 count)

- 2 tbsp. of Chicken Stock

Directions:

- Your air fryer should be set at 165°C. While you collect your ingredients, set a metal pan (6 x 3) inside of it to begin heating.

- Add the garlic, butter, & red pepper flakes to a heated 6-inch pan.

- Cook for two minutes while stirring only once, or till the butter has melted. Don't

miss this procedure. Everything tastes so nice because the butter has been infused with garlic as a result.

- Turn on the air fryer, then add the ingredients listed in the order given— butter, lemon juice, minced garlic, chives, red pepper flakes, chicken stock, basil, and shrimp—gently stirring between each addition.

- Cook the shrimp for five minutes, stirring once. The butter should now be completely melted and liquid, coating the shrimp with delicious flavour.

- Combine well, remove the six-inch pan with silicone gloves, and let it sit on the counter for a minute. By doing this, you prevent the shrimp from unintentionally overcooking and becoming rubbery by letting it cook in the residual heat.

- Stir for 1 minute. At this stage, the shrimp must be well cooked.

- Add more fresh basil leaves; enjoy.

Nutritional values per serving:

Total Calories: 221kcal, **Fats:** 13g, **Carbohydrates:** 1g, **Protein:** 23g

21. Lime Garlic Shrimp Skewers

Ready in: 13 mins.

Serves: 2

Difficulty: easy

Ingredients:

- 1 clove of garlic

- 1 cup of raw shrimp

- 1 lime

- freshly ground black pepper

- 1/8 tsp. of salt

- 5 wooden skewers (6-inch)

Directions:

- Soak wooden skewers for 20 minutes in water.

- Thaw frozen shrimp. Turn the Air Fryer on at 175°C.

- Combine shrimp with minced garlic & lime juice. Including salt and pepper.
- Thread shrimp onto each skewer. Place 8 minutes in the air fryer, flipping halfway through.
- Top with chopped cilantro and your preferred dip before serving.

Nutritional values per serving:

Total Calories: 76kcal, **Fats:** 0g, **Carbohydrates:** 4g, **Protein:** 13g

22. French Classic Mussels
Ready in: 12 mins.

Serves: 4

Difficulty: easy

Ingredients:

- 2 tbsp. of garlic minced
- 1 pound of mussels
- 4 tbsp. of butter melted & unsalted
- 2 tbsp. of heavy cream
- 2 tbsp. of dry white wine

Directions:

- Place the mussels in a large bowl and stir in the butter, garlic, white wine, & heavy cream.
- Place the mussels in the basket or on the rack.
- Set the oven to 205°C for 5 minutes, then shake or toss the basket with them. Set for a further two to five minutes.

Nutritional values per serving:

Total Calories: 97kcal, **Fats:** 5g, **Carbohydrates:** 5g, **Protein:** 8g

23. Garlic Butter Lobster Tails
Ready in: 10 mins.

Serves: 4

Difficulty: easy

Ingredients:

- 6 tbsp. of butter melted
- 4 lobster tails, take the meat out from shell, keep it adhered at the base & place it on the top of shelf.
- 1 tbsp. of packed cilantro, some more to garnish (or you can use any of the other greens as chives or parsley)
- 1 tsp. of Dijon mustard
- 2 cloves of garlic
- 2 tbsp. of lemon juice
- Some salt & black pepper
- 1/8 tsp. of creole seasoning

Directions:

- With the exception of the lobster tails, mix all the ingredients in a blender. Divide sauce into 2 bowls.
- Turn the air fryer on at 195°C. Place the lobster tails in the air fryer, coat them with half of garlic butter sauce, cover the lid, and cook for 5 to 7 minutes, or till the lobster is well cooked.
- Drizzle the heated lobsters with the remaining garlic butter, then top with fresh cilantro. Serve with mashed potatoes & a cucumber salad.

Nutritional values per serving:

Total Calories: 204kcal, **Fats:** 18g, Carbohydrates: 1g, **Protein:** 11g

24. Chili & Garlic Baby Octopus
Ready in: 40 mins.

Serves: 6

Difficulty: medium

Ingredients:

- 12 prawns (large), deveined and peeled (fresh or frozen)
- 8 baby octopus, whole (fresh or frozen)
- 4 garlic cloves, minced
- 1 tbsp. of olive oil
- 1 tsp. of chilli flakes

- Salt to taste

For salad:

- 125g of halved grape tomatoes
- 60g of lettuce leaves, mixed
- 2 Spring onions sprigs, chopped
- Half Spanish onion, sliced and quartered

For dressing:

- Olive oil
- 1 cup of chimichurri sauce

Directions:

- Toss the frozen prawns, baby octopus, chopped garlic, chilli flakes, olive oil, and salt in a big dish. Preheat the air fryer to 180°C. Thoroughly blend
- Put prawns and seasoned baby octopus in the air fryer. Cook for 12 minutes at 180 °C.
- When finished, remove.

For salad:

- Toss the ingredients for the salad in a big bowl.
- To the salad, add half a cup of chimichurri sauce.
- Depending on how much olive oil is already in your chimichurri sauce, you may need to add a little additional. If there is enough to incorporate into the salad, you won't need any.
- Combine salad and sauce.

To serve:

- Add prawns and tiny octopus to the salad as garnish.
- Spoon the leftover chimichurri sauce over the prawns and baby octopus.
- Dish out and savour!

Nutritional values per serving:

Total Calories: 60kcal, **Fats:** 1g, **Carbohydrates:** 7g, **Protein:** 5g

25. Charred Baby Octopus
Ready in: 30 mins.

Serves: 6

Difficulty: medium

Ingredients:

- 1 big Onion piece, diced
- 6 Baby Octopus pieces
- 1 diced carrot, small
- 1 slice of Lemon
- 2 tbsp. of Teriyaki Sauce
- 1 tsp. of sesame oil
- 6 pieces of wooden skewers
- Dash of black pepper

Directions:

- Bring some water to boil in a saucepan. Baby octopus should be added, parboiled for 3 minutes, and then the heat should be turned off. Drain thoroughly after removing the baby octopus.
- Olive oil, salt, and pepper are used to season sliced onion and carrots.
- The six wooden skewers should be soaked in warm water.
- Marinate the octopus for three to four hours in the refrigerator with sesame oil, teriyaki sauce, and a sprinkle of pepper.
- Take out of the fridge, skewer marinated baby octopus in between pieces of carrot and onion.
- Air-fry lemons and octopus skewers for approximately five minutes at 190°C on a well-oiled grill or skillet.
- Enjoy right now with your preferred dipping sauce or chilli.

Nutritional values per serving:

Total Calories: 45kcal, **Fats:** 1.5g, **Carbohydrates:** 1g, **Protein:** 7g

Chapter 8: Air Fried Diabetic Diet ~ Vegetarian Recipes

1. Honey Brussels Sprouts

Ready in: 23 mins.

Serves: 6

Difficulty: easy

Ingredients:

- 1 tbsp. of olive oil
- 1 pound of halved Brussels sprouts
- 1 tsp. of kosher salt
- 1/4 cup of garlic chilli paste
- 1 tsp. of white pepper
- 1 tbsp. of honey
- Sesame seeds, to garnish
- 2 tbsp. of water

Directions:

- In a big bowl, combine the salt, olive oil, and pepper, and toss Brussels sprouts to coat them evenly.

- Put Brussels sprouts in the air fryer's basket; they don't have to be arranged in a single layer, but doing so will make them extra crispy. Cook the sprouts in batches. For nine minutes, set your air fryer up to 195°C. Shake the basket & cook for an extra nine minutes after the allotted time has passed.

- In a small bowl, combine the honey, garlic chilli paste, and two tbsp. of water. For one mins or till the sauce is hot, place the bowl into the microwave and cook while covered.

- When Brussels sprouts are finished cooking, transfer them to a large bowl and immediately combine them with the sauce.

- Sprinkle sesame seeds on top. To get the crispiest results, serve right away.

Nutritional values per serving:

Total Calories: 77kcal, **Fats:** 3g, **Carbohydrates:** 13g, **Protein:** 2g

2. Air Fried Tofu

Ready in: 1 hr. 20 mins.

Serves: 4

Difficulty: medium

Ingredients:

- 1/3 cup of soy sauce, low sodium
- 16 ounces of extra-firm tofu
- 1/4 cup of rice vinegar
- 1 tbsp. of grated ginger
- 1 1/2 tbsp. of canola oil (or any other oil, neutral flavour)
- 1 tbsp. of brown sugar
- 1 1/2 tsp. of minced garlic
- 2 tsp. of sesame oil, toasted
- 1 tbsp. of green onions (sliced) to garnish (optional)

Directions:

- Place the tofu on a baking sheet with a rim and cover it with a fresh kitchen towel. Alternatively, spread some paper towels over the tofu and cover it. Put some heavy objects on the top of the tofu, such as a pan, a big book, or a chopping board, to weigh it all down. This will assist in pressing the tofu's extra moisture out. Give the tofu roughly 30 minutes to stand.

- In a separate bowl, combine the vinegar, soy sauce, canola oil, brown sugar, ginger, sesame oil, & garlic while the tofu is still standing.

- Tofu marinade into a bowl with a whisk

- Cubes of pressed tofu should be cut into 1-inch pieces and put in a baking dish (shallow) or another nonreactive container.

- Place diced extra-firm pressed tofu into a dish

- Over the tofu, pour the marinade mixture. Refrigerate the dish with a cover for 30 mins–1 hour.

- Turn the air fryer on at 195°C. The tofu cubes should be arranged in the basket of the air fryer & cooked until crisp for 12-15 minutes, flipping them over every 3-4 minutes.

- Put tofu from an air fryer in a little serving dish.

- The tofu cubes may be served hot or cold.

Nutritional values per serving:

Total Calories: 125kcal, Fats: 3g, Carbohydrates: 2g, Protein: 3g

3. Roasted Bell Peppers
Ready in: 12 mins.

Serves: 2

Difficulty: easy

Ingredients:

- 2 tsp. of oil, avocado or coconut

- 3 Bell peppers (any colour)

- ¼ tsp. of salt

- 1 heaped tsp. of taco seasoning

- ¼ tsp. of white or black pepper

Directions:

- After washing the bell peppers, you can dry them using a paper towel or a clean kitchen towel. Now split them in half, remove the seeds, and cut them into cubes or long or short strips, as you choose. Keep in mind that depending on size you cut them, the time of your air frying may vary significantly.

- Place the diced bell peppers in a bowl and season with taco spice, salt, and pepper.

- Fill your air fryer with the seasoned bell peppers, being careful not to overcrowd them. For the feature of air frying to function properly, it is crucial to provide room between the pieces.

- Now, air-fry them for 10-12 minutes at 195°C. If you first place the pieces correctly with sufficient space between them, there is no need to toss the basket halfway through. If you prefer the chargrilled appearance, you may even roast a bit longer.

Nutritional values per serving:

Total Calories: 74kcal, Fats: 4.3g, Carbohydrates: 9.2g, Protein: 1.3g

4. Air fried Pickles
Ready in: 20 mins.

Serves: 6

Difficulty: medium

Ingredients:

- 1 cup of flour

- 2 cups of hamburger pickles (sliced)

- 1 tbsp. of garlic powder

- ½ tbsp. of Cayenne pepper

- 1 tbsp. of Cajun seasoning

- Olive oil

Directions:

- Before starting, place the pickles on a piece of paper towel to assist to drain any extra pickle juice. This will help the flour mixture adhere to the pickles more effectively.

- Combine the flour, Cajun spice, garlic powder, and cayenne pepper in a medium bowl.

- Coat all sides of the pickles by dipping them into the flour mixture.

- Rub both sides with olive oil.

- Arrange the pickles into the air fryer in a single layer, being careful to keep them from touching.

- Cook for 10 minutes at 205°C. Cook for five more minutes after flipping.

Nutritional values per serving:

Total Calories: 55kcal, Fats: 1.3g, Carbohydrates: 8.7g, Protein: 2.4g

5. Zucchini Pizza

Ready in: 20 mins.

Serves: 4

Difficulty: medium

Ingredients:

- salt and black pepper
- 1 zucchini (medium), sliced into ¼" rounds
- ½ cup of pizza sauce
- pepperoni, in small pieces (optional)
- ½ cup of mozzarella cheese, shredded
- Black olives (sliced), cut into small pieces (optional)

Directions:

- Cut the zucchini lengthwise into 1/4" rounds, then season with salt & pepper. For two minutes, preheat your air fryer at 175°C.
- Put seasoned zucchini slices on top
- Use nonstick spray to coat the air fryer basket, then gently add as many slices of zucchini as will fit within. Cook for 4 minutes at 175°C.
- Take each zucchini slice out of the air fryer using tongs. Pizza sauce, pepperoni, cheese, and olives are placed on top of each slice.
- Reposition the slices into the air fryer & cook for an additional 4-5 minutes at 175°C. Use the tongs to remove the pizza bits from the air fryer, then let them cool before eating.

Nutritional values per serving:

Total Calories: 59kcal, **Fats:** 0g, **Carbohydrates:** 0g, **Protein:** 0g

6. Shishito Peppers

Ready in: 15 mins.

Serves: 4

Difficulty: easy

Ingredients:

- avocado oil cooking spray
- 8 ounces of shishito peppers
- salt, to taste

Directions:

- Wash and well dry the peppers before cooking. Don't take the stems off. Leave the shishito peppers' stems on.
- Spray them with avocado oil after they have been cleaned and dried. They are now prepared for the air fryer.
- Shishito peppers should be arranged in one single layer into the air fryer's basket or tray.
- Heat the air fryer up to 205°C for cooking. A timer for 7-8 minutes has been set.
- There isn't any need to wait for it to heat up before adding the peppers. The ideal amount of time for air frying is 8 minutes, plus roughly 2-3 minutes for preheating.
- They could hiss and pop as they cooked. That's okay; they should just expand while they cook rather than explode.
- They are prepared when the timer sounds. They need to have black burned spots and blisters.
- Use tongs to carefully transfer them to a dish or bowl.
- Add salt to them as required. Immediately serve as it is or with the preferred dipping sauces.

Nutritional values per serving:

Total Calories: 45kcal, **Fats:** 3.5g, **Carbohydrates:** 3g, **Protein:** 1g

7. Onion Bites

Ready in: 25 mins.

Serves: 2

Difficulty: medium

Ingredients:

- 1 4th cup of gram flour, plus add some more if required

- 1 red onion (large), sliced lengthwise
- 1 tbsp. of rice flour
- 1-2 finely chopped green chillies
- 1 tsp. ginger grated
- 1 stalk of finely chopped curry leaves
- ¼ tsp. of carrom seeds
- 1 4th cup of finely chopped coriander leaves
- ¼ tsp. of turmeric
- ½ tsp. garam masala
- ½ tsp. of chilli powder (red)
- ½ tbsp. of hot oil
- oil to air fry
- half tsp. of salt

Directions:

- Thinly slice one big red onion (approximately 250 grams). They should not be very thick or thin.

- Place the thinly sliced onions in a big bowl. To a mixing bowl, add all the things except the gram flour, rice flour, and oil. With your fingers, rub the onions gently.

- Let the bowl rest for 10 minutes with a plate on top to assist the onions release moisture.

- Add rice flour and gram flour after 10 minutes. Mix well to get a firm, non-soggy mixture. The moisture from the onions must be enough to create the dough; do not add any more water. Add 1/2 tbsp. of heated oil next. Onion bites remain soft on the inside as a result of this. Don't skip it.

- Set air fryer at 205°C. Add onion mixture in batches into the air fryer and let it cook for 10 minutes.

Nutritional values per serving:

Total Calories: 140kcal, **Fats:** 5g, **Carbohydrates:** 20g, **Protein:** 5g

8. Paneer Tikka Fry

Ready in: 50 mins.

Serves: 4

Difficulty: medium

Ingredients:

Tikka Marinade Masala:

- 1 tbsp. of chickpea flour (or gram flour)
- ½ cup of Greek yogurt
- 1 tbsp. of garlic ginger paste
- 1 tsp. red chilli powder
- ¼ tsp. of turmeric powder
- ½ tsp. cumin powder
- ½ tsp. garam masala
- 1 tsp. of chaat masala powder
- 1 tsp. of dried fenugreek leaves
- one tbsp. of oil
- 1 tsp. of lemon juice
- Some salt

Other things:

- 1-2 bell peppers, medium (mix of red, green, and yellow) in 1-inch cubes
- 300 grams of Paneer (about two cups) cut in 1-inch cubes
- 1 red onion (medium) cut in 1-inch cubes

Garnish:

- slices of onion
- lemon wedges
- mint sauce
- chaat masala

Directions:

- Combine the Greek yoghurt, gram flour, garlic-ginger paste, cumin powder, turmeric powder, red chilli powder, fenugreek seeds, chaat masala, salt, lemon juice, & oil in a large bowl.

- Include the bell peppers, onion, and Paneer. To coat, well, toss. Cover the bowl

& place in the refrigerator for 30 minutes at least or up to 1 day. To avoid burning, whether using an air fryer, oven, or grill, soak the wooden skewers into cold water for 10 minutes at least.

- Using a skewer, carefully thread Paneer, bell peppers, and onions in alternation. Assemble the remaining skewers in a similar manner.

- Set the air fryer's temperature to 180°C. Place each prepared skewer in the basket, spacing them out 1/2 inch apart. Oil should be brushed or sprayed on top to prevent the Paneer and vegetables from drying out.

- Do 5 minutes of cooking at 180°C. The skewers should be turned after 5 minutes, brushed or gently sprayed with oil, and cooked for a further 2~3 minutes.

- Remove to a serving dish, pour some lime juice over it, top with chaat masala, and serve right away with mint chutney.

Nutritional values per serving:

Total Calories: 293kcal, Fats: 23g, Carbohydrates: 8g, Protein: 14g

9. Cauliflower Manchurian

Ready in: 30 mins.

Serves: 2

Difficulty: medium

Ingredients:

For Batter:

- ¼ cup of corn flour/corn starch
- 2 ~ 2.5 cups of cauliflower, cut in florets (almost about 20 to 22 florets)
- ¼ cup Of all-purpose flour
- 2 tsp. of ginger-garlic paste
- one tsp. of red chilli powder
- 2 tsp. of tomato ketchup
- Some water
- salt & pepper to taste

For Sauce:

- 1 tsp. of ginger minced
- 1 tbsp. of oil
- 1 tsp. of garlic minced
- ¼ cup of bell pepper
- ½ cup of finely chopped onion
- 1 tbsp. of soy sauce
- ¼ cup of tomato Sauce
- 2 tsp. of red chilli sauce
- 1 tbsp. of white distilled vinegar
- 2 tbsp. of finely chopped spring/green onion
- 2 tbsp. of finely chopped cilantro
- salt to taste

Directions:

For Batter:

- Combine all the ingredients listed under "batter" and add some water at a time to the mixture to get a pancake consistency.

- Ensure that the batter is smooth and free of lumps.

Frying Cauliflower Florets:

- Include cauliflower florets in the batter, and deep-fry until golden and crisp.

- Only add 7 to 8 florets at one time; do not overcrowd.

- Once all of the florets are mature. On paper towels, set them aside.

Manchurian Sauce:

- Add the ginger and garlic to the hot, Smokey oil and cook for 20 seconds.

- Include onion and pepper as well. Cook for 30 to 90 seconds.

- After adding the vinegar, continue tossing the mixture while adding each sauce one at a time.

- After adding the vinegar, continue tossing the mixture while adding each sauce one at a time.

- Add fried cauliflower florets last, season with salt (if necessary), and combine for two minutes. Add spring onions & coriander/cilantro. After one last toss, serve it right away with tomato ketchup.

- To prepare Gobi Manchurian into an air fryer, dunk the florets into the batter and arrange them in a single layer on the air fryer's tray.

- Apply some oil to the basket of the air fryer using a brush or spray. For 12 to 15 minutes, or till they are browned & crispy, air fried them in an air fryer that has been set to 200°C. Shake them once you've finished.

Nutritional values per serving:

Total Calories: 236kcal, Fats: 16g, Carbohydrates: 22g, Protein: 3.1g

10. Tandoori Potatoes

Ready in: 1 hr.

Serves: 4

Difficulty: medium

Ingredients:

Tikka Marinade:

- 1 tbsp. of chickpea flour (or gram flour)
- ½ cup of Greek yogurt
- 1 tbsp. of garlic ginger paste
- 1 tsp. red chilli powder
- ¼ tsp. turmeric powder
- ½ tsp. cumin powder
- ½ tsp. garam masala
- one tsp. chaat masala powder
- 1 tsp. dried fenugreek leaves
- one tbsp. of oil
- 1 tsp. of lemon juice
- salt to taste

Other Ingredients:

- 1 bell pepper, medium (yellow or red), cut in 1-inch cubes

- 1 pound of baby potatoes (around 16)
- 1 red onion (medium), cut in 1-inch cubes

Garnish:

- onion slices
- lemon wedges
- mint sauce
- chaat masala

Directions:

- The baby potatoes must first be parboiled. The baby potatoes may be parboiled in an Instant Pot at High Pressure for ~12 minutes, followed by a Natural Pressure Release, or they can be pressure cooked in a stovetop pressure cooker for 1 whistle.

- After that, thoroughly drain the potatoes, wipe them dry using a kitchen towel, and remove the skin.

Making a Marinade:

- Hung curd, gram flour, ginger-garlic paste, red chile, turmeric, cumin, chaat masala, garam masala, fenugreek seeds, salt, lemon juice, and oil should all be combined in a big bowl.

- Add the onion, bell peppers, and baby potatoes that have been parboiled. To coat, well, toss. Refrigerate for about 1 day or 30 minutes at least with the bowl covered in the fridge.

- In the meanwhile, immerse wooden skewers in the cold water for 10 minutes at least to avoid scorching if using an oven, grill, or air fryer.

- Using a skewer, carefully thread potatoes, onions and bell peppers in alternation. Prepare the rest of the skewers in a similar manner.

- Set the air fryer's temperature to 180°C. Place each prepared skewer in the basket, spacing them out 12 inches apart. Oil may be brushed or sprayed on top to prevent the potato and vegetables from drying out.

- Do 15 minutes of cooking at 180°C. Turn the skewers after 10 minutes, roast for a further 5 minutes, then gently spritz or brush with oil.

Nutritional values per serving:

Total Calories: 164kcal, **Fats:** 4g, **Carbohydrates:** 26g, **Protein:** 6g

11. Stuffed Okra
Ready in: 22 mins.

Serves: 4

Difficulty: medium

Ingredients:

- 2 tbsp. of oil (1 to 2 tsp. to air fry)
- 230 grams of okra (about 20 to 22)

Stuffing Masala:

- 1 tbsp. of coriander powder
- three tbsp. of roasted peanut powder
- 1 tsp. of cumin powder
- 1 tsp. of red chilli powder
- ¼ tsp. of turmeric powder
- half tsp. of garam masala
- ½ tsp. of fennel powder, optional
- ½ tsp. of lime juice
- 2 tsp. of oil
- salt to taste

Directions:

- Okra should first be rinsed and dried with a fresh towel. Trim the okra's top and bottom portions. Slit in the middle.
- For preparing the stuffing masala, take a small bowl and add salt, lime juice, coriander powder, roasted peanut powder, red chilli powder, cumin powder, turmeric powder, & garam masala. Mix thoroughly.
- After that, add a spoonful of oil and thoroughly mix. When stuffing the okra, oil is applied to assist the spices in adhering.
- Fill the okra with the prepared masala and set it aside. If necessary, remove the big seeds from the okra before filling.
- Set the air fryer's temperature to 180°C. Spread the filled okra in a single layer in the basket of air fryer (cook in batches if required). Spray or gently brush some oil on the surface.
- Air fry them for 10 to 12 minutes at 180°C. Flip the okra after around 8 minutes and remove the basket. If the stuffed okra seems to be dry, brush some oil over it.
- Take out stuffed okra from the air fryer, and serve with a slice of lime on the side.

Nutritional values per serving:

Total Calories: 166kcal, **Fats:** 15g, **Carbohydrates:** 7g, **Protein:** 3g

12. Roasted Cauliflower Potatoes
Ready in: 30 mins.

Serves: 4

Difficulty: medium

Ingredients:

- 2 Potatoes (small), cut in ¾" pieces (almost about 1 cup)
- 1 Cauliflower head (medium) cut in florets (almost about 3 cups)
- 2-3 tbsp. of Olive Oil
- 1 Green Chili, cut lengthwise
- 1 tbsp. of minced Ginger-Garlic
- 1 Onion sliced (medium), about ¾ to 1 cup
- 1 tbsp. of Lime juice
- 1 diced Tomato, medium (about half cup)
- 2 tbsp. of Coriander leaves to garnish

Spices:

- ½ tsp. of Turmeric powder
- ½ tsp. of Red chilli powder
- ½ tsp. of Cumin powder

- ½ tsp. of Garam masala
- 1 tsp. of Coriander powder
- Salt to taste

Directions:

- Combine the cauliflower, potato, onions, tomatoes, green chillies, minced ginger, garlic, and oil in a large mixing basin.
- For three to four minutes, preheat your air fryer to 195°C.
- Next, if desired, lightly oil the air fryer plate, and then lay the potato-cauliflower mixture out in one single layer (do not cram it on there).
- Place for 12–15 minutes at 195°C in an air fryer. At the midway point, shake the basket.
- Add some cilantro and lime juice as a garnish. Serve warm.

Nutritional values per serving:

Total Calories: 191kcal, Fats: 8g, Carbohydrates: 28g, Protein: 5g

13. Tandoori Cauliflower

Ready in: 35 mins.

Serves: 4

Difficulty: medium

Ingredients:

For Marinade:

- 1 tbsp. of chickpea flour (or gram flour)
- ½ cup of Greek yogurt
- 1 tbsp. of garlic ginger paste
- 1 tsp. of red chilli powder
- ¼ tsp. of turmeric powder
- ½ tsp. of cumin powder
- ½ tsp. of garam masala
- 1 tsp. of chaat masala powder
- 1 tsp. of dried fenugreek leaves
- 1 tbsp. of oil
- 1 tsp. of lemon juice

- salt to taste

Vegetables:

- 1 cauliflower (medium), about 18-20 florets

Garnish:

- onion slices
- lemon wedges
- mint sauce
- chaat masala

Directions:

- Clean, then slice the whole head of cauliflower into about equal-sized bite-sized florets for uniform cooking.
- Combine hanging curd, gram flour, turmeric powder, ginger-garlic paste, cumin powder, red chilli powder, fenugreek seeds, chaat masala, salt, lemon juice, and oil in a big bowl.
- After that, stir in the cauliflower florets to thoroughly coat each one in the marinade. For 15 to 20 minutes, cover the bowl & place it in the fridge.
- Set the air fryer's temperature to 180°C. Spread out the marinated florets of cauliflower in a single layer in the basket of the air fryer (cook in batches if required). Oil may be brushed or sprayed on top.
- Air fry them for 14–18 minutes, or until the edges begin to crisp and brown, at 180°C. At the midway point, shake the basket.
- Remove to a serving dish, pour some lime juice over it, top with chaat masala, and serve right away with mint sauce.

Nutritional values per serving:

Total Calories: 96kcal, Fats: 4g, Carbohydrates: 10g, Protein: 6g

14. Tofu Tikka

Ready in: 55 mins.

Serves: 6

Difficulty: medium

Ingredients:

For Marinade:

- 1 tbsp. of chickpea flour (or gram flour)
- ½ cup of Greek yogurt
- 1 tbsp. of garlic ginger paste
- 1 tsp. of red chilli powder
- ¼ tsp. of turmeric powder
- ½ tsp. of cumin powder
- ½ tsp. of garam masala
- 1 tsp. of chaat masala powder
- 1 tsp. of dried fenugreek leaves
- 1 tbsp. of oil
- 1 tsp. of lemon juice
- salt to taste

Other Ingredients:

- 1-2 medium bell peppers (mix of green, red, and yellow) cut into 1-inch cubes
- 16 oz. extra-firm tofu pressed for 30 minutes, cut into 1" cubes
- 1 small red onion cut into 1-inch cubes

Garnish:

- onion slices
- lemon wedges
- mint sauce
- chaat masala

Directions:

- For 30 minutes at least, press the tofu with any heavy objects. It will remove the extra moisture.
- The tofu should then be diced.
- Mix together in a sizable bowl the hanging curd, gram flour, turmeric powder, ginger-garlic paste, red chilli powder, chaat masala, roasted cumin powder, garam masala, lemon juice, fenugreek seeds, salt, and oil. Mix everything well.
- After that, include bell peppers, tofu cubes, and onions. Gently toss the tofu and vegetables to cover them evenly.
- Place the bowl in the refrigerator for 30 minutes at least and up to 1 day with the lid on.
- In the meanwhile, soak bamboo skewers or toothpicks in water for 15 minutes least to prevent scorching.
- On a toothpick, delicately thread the tofu, onion and bell peppers.
- Set the air fryer's temperature to 200°C. Make cautious not to crowd the prepped toothpicks or skewers as you arrange them. To prevent the tofu and vegetables from drying out, spray or brush some oil on top.
- Do 5 minutes of cooking at 200°C. Turn the toothpicks/skewers after 5 minutes, cook for a further 3 to 4 minutes, and then gently brush or spritz with oil.
- Transfer to a serving platter, squeeze lime juice over it, top with chaat masala, and serve the air-fried tofu tikka right away with the mint sauce.

Nutritional values per serving:

Total Calories: 11kcal, **Fats:** 0.1g, **Carbohydrates:** 3g, **Protein:** 0.4g

15. Air Fried Samosa

Ready in: 10 mins.

Serves: 4

Difficulty: easy

Ingredients:

- 1 tbsp. of oil
- 4 frozen samosas (large)

Directions:

- Set the air fryer's temperature to 193°C. In the air fryer basket, add the frozen samosas, allowing space between each one. The samosas' tops should be oiled with a spray or brush.

- Air fry them for 8 to 12 minutes, or until they are crisp and golden brown, at 193 °C. Using kitchen tongs, carefully turn the samosas halfway through.

- The size, brand of used frozen samosas, and air fryer will all affect how long they take to cook.

- Take the samosa out of the air fryer & serve it hot with your preferred chutney or dipping sauce. Such a treat!

Nutritional values per serving:

Total Calories: 155kcal, **Fats:** 8g, **Carbohydrates:** 15g, **Protein:** 5g

16. Beetroot Cutlet

Ready in: 30 mins.

Serves: 3

Difficulty: medium

Ingredients:

- 2 boiled & grated potatoes, medium (about 1 cup)

- 1 grated beetroot, large (about almost 1.25 cup)

- ¼ cup of roasted peanuts, crushed

- 1 tsp. of ginger grated

- 3 tbsp. of corn flour or bread crumbs or rice flour

- 2 finely chopped green chillies

- ½ tsp. of garam masala

- 2 tbsp. of finely chopped cilantro

- 1 tsp. of chat masala powder

- salt to taste

- ½ tsp. of lime juice

Directions:

- Boil the potatoes for 3–4 whistles on medium heat in a pan or pressure cooker with some salt and water.

- Mash or Grate the potatoes after finishing.

- Beets should be peeled, grated, and their surplus juice squeezed out.

- The beets in this recipe have not been cooked.

- Take a bowl for mixing. Mix all the ingredients together well. As a binding agent, you may instead use rice flour or corn flour in place of the breadcrumbs. If the mixture is too wet, add additional bread crumbs.

- Use a tsp. of oil to grease your hand to prevent the mixture from sticking.

- Create a ball about the size of a lemon, flatten it between the palms, and then shape it into a cutlet. Repeat the procedure with the leftover mixture to create additional cutlets.

- Put some parchment paper or aluminium foil that has been gently greased in the basket or tray.

- Place cutlets in a single layer at this point.

- Set the temperature up to 190°C in an air fryer, choose the duration to be 12 minutes.

- Place the tray in the air fryer. Carefully turn the cutlets after an interval

- Beetroot cutlets should be served hot with mint sauce or ketchup after they are crispy & golden brown.

Nutritional values per serving:

Total Calories: 271kcal, **Fats:** 7g, **Carbohydrates:** 46g, **Protein:** 9g

17. Crispy Corn Fritters

Ready in: 20 mins.

Serves: 2

Difficulty: medium

Ingredients:

- ½ finely chopped onion

- 1 cup of corn kernels (sweet), boiled & crushed coarsely

- ¼ cup of gram flour or chickpea flour
- 2-3 finely chopped green chillies
- 1 tbsp. of rice flour
- ¼ tsp. of turmeric
- 1 tsp. of garam masala powder
- 1 tsp. of garlic ginger paste
- ¼ cup of finely chopped cilantro
- ½ tsp. of cumin
- few chopped curry leaves
- Some oil
- salt to taste

Directions:

- The boiling sweet corn kernels should be ground coarsely. Use a mixer or blender to pulse a few times.

- Combine the roughly crushed sweet corn with the onions, ginger-garlic paste, green chillies, turmeric, coriander leaves, chat masala powder, gram flour, cumin, rice flour, & salt in a large bowl.

- Combine and thoroughly blend without adding water. If needed, add extra gram of flour.

- Set the air fryer to 200°C for 3–4 minutes.

- Fill the basket with a layer of aluminium foil or parchment paper, gently oil it, and add the corn fritter mixture. Fry the fritters for 10 to 12 minutes, rotating them halfway through.

Nutritional values per serving:

Total Calories: 104kcal, Fats: 1g, Carbohydrates: 21g, Protein: 3g

18. Tandoori Broccoli
Ready in: 40 mins.

Serves: 4

Difficulty: medium

Ingredients:
For Marinade:

- 1 tbsp. of chickpea flour (or gram flour)

- ½ cup of Greek yogurt
- 1 tbsp. of garlic ginger paste
- 1 tsp. of red chilli powder
- 1 4th tsp. of turmeric powder
- ½ tsp. of cumin powder
- ½ tsp. of garam masala
- 1 tsp. of chaat masala powder
- 1 tsp. of dried fenugreek leaves
- one tbsp. of oil
- 1 tsp. of lemon juice
- salt to taste

Other Ingredients:

- 1 head of broccoli, large (about 20 to 22 florets, medium-sized)

Garnish:

- onion slices
- lemon wedges
- mint sauce
- chaat masala

Directions:

- To ensure consistent cooking, clean and slice the head of broccoli in bite-sized florets.

- The broccoli must be blanched in the next step. Using high heat, bring a pot (medium-sized) of salted water to boil. Broccoli should be cooked for one minute in boiling water before being transferred to a bowl of ice cubes and water. Cubes.

- After they have cooled, remove the water from them and use a paper or kitchen towel to pat them dry. Or you may use your Instant Pot to steam the broccoli.

- Combine hanging curd, grammes flour, ginger-garlic paste, cumin powder, red chilli powder, turmeric powder, fenugreek seeds, chaat masala, salt, lemon juice, and oil in a large bowl.

- After that, stir in the broccoli florets that have been blanched or steam-cooked until each one is well covered in the marinade. For 15 to 20 minutes, cover the bowl & place it in the fridge.

- Set the air fryer's temperature to 180°C. Spread the marinated florets of broccoli in a single layer in the basket of the air fryer (cook in batches if required). The broccoli won't dry out if some oil is brushed or sprayed on the top.

- Air fry for 8–10 minutes at 180°C or until the edges begin to brown and become crispy. At the midway point, shake the basket.

- Take it out onto a serving platter, sprinkle with chaat masala, squeeze lime juice over it, and serve it right away with mint sauce.

Nutritional values per serving:

Total Calories: 108kcal, Fats: 4g, Carbohydrates: 12g, Protein: 7g

19. Cottage Cheese Popcorn

Ready in: 25 mins.

Serves: 3

Difficulty: medium

Ingredients:

- 1 tsp. of ginger garlic paste
- 1 cup of cottage cheese (1-inch cubes)
- ½ tsp. of chilli powder (red)
- ½ tsp. of mixed dried herbs
- ½ tsp. of garam masala powder
- 1 4th tsp. of pepper powder
- 2 tsp. of oil for spraying
- ¼ cup of refined flour or corn flour
- salt to taste

For Crust:

- ¼ tsp. of red chilli powder
- ½ cup of bread crumbs
- ⅛ tsp. of salt

Directions:

- Ginger garlic paste, garam masala, red chilli powder, pepper powder, mixed herbs, and salt should be added to a bowl. Then mix thoroughly before adding the cottage cheese.

- To produce a paste, use 1/4 cup of maize flour and add as much water as is necessary.

- Combine salt, red chilli powder, and breadcrumbs; set aside.

- Next, dip the cheese cubes in the paste, shake off any excess batter, and fully cover each cheese cube with the bread crumbs mixture. For 15 minutes at least, refrigerate.

- Coat the fryer basket and the cheese cubes with the cooking spray, and then put the bread-coated cheese cubes in the fryer basket in a single layer.

- Popcorn should be cooked for 6 minutes at 190°C. It should take another 5 minutes to brown and crisp after flipping. If you believe the food is not fully done, stir it and cook it for two more minutes. With the remaining cheese popcorn, repeat.

- Remove the popcorn from the fryer and place it on a serving platter. Serve right away with your preferred dipping sauce.

Nutritional values per serving:

Total Calories: 290kcal, Fats: 18g, Carbohydrates: 17g, Protein: 12g

20. Cajun Potatoes

Ready in: 25 mins.

Serves: 2

Difficulty: medium

Ingredients:

Cajun Mayonnaise:

- 1 tsp. garlic powder
- 4 tbsp. of mayonnaise
- 1 tsp. onion powder

- ½ tsp. of thyme (dried)
- ½ tsp. of dried oregano
- ½ tsp. ground black pepper
- 2 tbsp. of milk (optional)
- 1 tsp. of red chilli powder
- 1 tsp. of tomato ketchup
- salt to taste

Crispy Potatoes:

- 2 tbsp. of corn flour
- 10 to 12 baby potatoes
- oil
- salt to taste
- 1 tbsp. of finely chopped coriander leaves
- 2 tbsp. of finely chopped onions

Directions:

Preparing Mayonnaise Dressing:

- In a bowl, combine the tomato ketchup, mayonnaise, and all of the spices listed under "Cajun Mayonnaise Ingredients."
- Place aside. 1-2 tbsp. of milk may be added if the dressing is very thick.
- Getting the Potatoes Ready:
- Cleanse the potatoes to remove any debris.
- Boil the potatoes until they are just soft (90 percent cooked).
- Next, set the potatoes onto a cutting board and pound each tiny potato with a hefty spoon until the skin slightly breaks (do not break).
- Sprinkle some cornflour over the potatoes, then toss them to evenly cover all sides.
- Fill the air fryer basket with the floured baby potatoes in a single layer at this point. Apply some oil to the potatoes' surface.
- Place the potatoes on the platter after they are crispy & golden brown.

- Lastly, arrange the fried potatoes on a platter for serving. On each potato, sprinkle coriander, finely chopped onions, and Cajun Mayonnaise.

Nutritional values per serving:

Total Calories: 253kcal, **Fats:** 8g, **Carbohydrates:** 43g, **Protein:** 5g

21. Vegetable Chilli Cheese Toast
Ready in: 15 mins.

Serves: 4

Difficulty: easy

Ingredients:

- 1 cup of mozzarella cheese, shredded
- 4 bread (white or brown)
- ¼ cup of coloured (any) bell peppers
- 1-2 finely chopped jalapeno or green chillies
- 2 tbsp. of tomato, finely chopped (deseeded)
- 1 tsp. of garlic, minced
- ½ tsp. of oregano (or any other mixed herbs)
- 1 tbsp. of finely chopped coriander leaves, optional
- salt & pepper, to taste

Directions:

- Dice or chop the veggies finely.
- In a mixing dish, combine the cheese, veggies, and seasonings. Set apart.
- Toast the bread on one side just with butter.
- On the toasted side of the bread, spread the chilli cheese mixture.
- Set the air fryer's temperature to 165°C. The bread slice should be cooked in the basket of air fryer at 165°C for 5 to 6 minutes, or until the cheese is melted and the top is beginning to brown. Continue by adding more slices.

Nutritional values per serving:

Total Calories: 169kcal, Fats: 8g, Carbohydrates: 16g, Protein: 9g

22. Bread Pizza

Ready in: 20 mins.

Serves: 2

Difficulty: medium

Ingredients:

- ½ cup of Pizza sauce
- 4 Slices of Bread
- 1 cup of Processed/Mozzarella Cheese, shredded
- ¼ cup of finely chopped onion
- ¼ cup of green bell peppers
- ¼ cup of tomato, finely chopped (deseeded)
- 2 tsp. of red chilli flakes
- 2 tsp. of pizza seasoning or any other mixed herbs
- Salt, to taste
- 2 tbsp. of butter

Directions:

- Spread some butter onto the pan and toast the bread until it is crisp and brown on one side.
- Spread your pizza sauce on the toasted bread, and toast the side up.
- Sprinkle some pizza seasoning, mozzarella cheese, onion, bell pepper, tomato, and chilli flakes.
- Set the air fryer's temperature to 165°C. Slices of bread pizza should be placed on the basket of air fryer and cooked for 7-8 minutes at 330°F, or till the cheese melts & the top is lightly browned. Continue by adding more slices.

Nutritional values per serving:

Total Calories: 130kcal, Fats: 4.1g, Carbohydrates: 18.2g, Protein: 5.5g

23. Veggie Bread Roll

Ready in: 45 mins.

Serves: 4

Difficulty: easy

Ingredients:

- ½ tsp. of salt
- 4 potatoes (medium-sized), peeled & chopped
- water as required

Spices:

- 1 tsp. of cumin seeds
- 1 tbsp. of olive oil
- 1-2 green chillies, chopped
- 1 tsp. of cumin powder
- 1 tsp. of coriander powder
- ½ tsp. of turmeric powder
- 1 tsp. of garam masala
- salt as needed
- 1 tbsp. of lime juice
- 12 slices of white bread
- ¼ cup of chopped cilantro

Directions:

- Potatoes should be boiled.
- In a sauté pan, heat the oil over medium heat. Fill the pan with oil.
- Add the cumin seeds to the heated oil. Green chillies should be added when they begin to sizzle. They need around 10 seconds of sautéing.
- Add salt, turmeric powder, garam masala, cumin powder, and coriander powder. After thoroughly combining, add the potatoes, lime juice, and cilantro right away.
- Mash the ingredients with a potato masher or the back of a spatula until there are no more lumps.
- Using a rolling pin, flatten the bread pieces one at a time.

- Place a flattened piece of bread on top of around 1.5 teaspoons of the potato filling.

- Form a long cylinder out of the firmly rolled bread pieces. To seal the bread's edges, dab them with water.

- Carry out the same procedure with the remaining bread pieces.

- Turn the air fryer on at 205°C. Allow it to warm up for approximately five minutes.

- Put the rolls into the basket and bake it at 205°C for about 10 minutes.

- Serve hot with ketchup or mint sauce.

Nutritional values per serving:

Total Calories: 244kcal, **Fats:** 4g, **Carbohydrates:** 44g, **Protein:** 8g

24. Eggplant Parmesan Pasta
Ready in: 45 mins.

Serves: 8

Difficulty: medium

Ingredients:

- 2 tbsp. of nutritional yeast, plus 1 tsp.

- 4 crispy bread crackers

- 1 tsp. of garlic powder

- ¼ cups of unflavored, unsweetened plant milk, like almond, cashew, soy, or rice

- 1 tsp. of Italian seasoning (dried), crushed

- 1 eggplant, medium (1 lb.), peeled & sliced in half-inch rounds

- 1 chopped onion (1 cup)

- 10 oz. of dry linguine (whole grain)

- 1 chopped green bell pepper (1 cup)

- 1 jar of marinara sauce, oil-free (22- to 23-oz.)

- 1 package of fresh button mushrooms, sliced (8-oz.)

- ¼ cup of fresh basil, chopped

- 1 can of no-salt-added tomatoes, diced (14.5-oz), undrained

Directions:

- Set air fryer to a 187°C temperature. Place crackers, 2 tablespoons of nutritional yeast, garlic powder, & Italian seasoning in a food processor. Place in a narrow bowl after processing until finely chopped undercover. Milk should be poured into another small dish. Each eggplant slice should be dipped into the milk, followed by the crumbs, to gently cover both sides. Set in a baking pan.

- If required, add the eggplant slices to the air fryer in stages so that they don't contact. Slices of eggplant should be air-fried for 12 to 15 minutes, or until they are soft and the breading is crunchy.

- Prepare the linguine in the meanwhile according to the instructions on the box. Drain and put the pot back. Cook bell pepper, onion, and mushrooms in a large pan over medium-high heat for 5-7 minutes or till soft stirring regularly & adding water, 1-2 Tbsp. At a time, as required to avoid sticking. Transfer to pasta-filled pot. Tomatoes and marinara sauce are added; combine thoroughly. Cook for 5 minutes, or until well heated.

- Add eggplant to the linguine mixture on top. Add the basil and the last teaspoon of nutritional yeast.

Nutritional values per serving:

Total Calories: 810 kcal, **Fats:** 29g, **Carbohydrates:** 110g, **Protein:** 31g

25. Kale & Sweet Potato Calzones
Ready in: 1hr. 30 mins.

Serves: 6

Difficulty: medium

Ingredients:

- 2¼ cups of potato flakes (or 3 tbsp. + ½ cup of potato flour)

- ⅓ cup of raw cashews

- 1 cup of whole wheat flour

- 2½ cups of white sweet potato (peeled), finely chopped

- ½ tsp. of sea salt
- 1 cup of onion, finely chopped
- 3 cloves of garlic, minced
- 1 cup of red bell pepper, coarsely chopped
- 1 tbsp. of fresh thyme, chopped (or 1 & ½ tsp. of dried crushed thyme)
- 2 cups of steamed kale, chopped
- 1 tbsp. of fresh oregano, chopped (or 1 & ½ tsp. of crushed dried oregano)
- 1 & ¼ cups of unflavored, unsweetened plant-based milk
- 1 tbsp. of white wine vinegar
- 6 tbsp. of nutritional yeast
- 1½ cups of marinara sauce (oil-free), warmed
- Red pepper (crushed), to taste

Directions:

- Soak the cashews in 1 & 1/2 cups of hot water for 20 minutes to make dough. Blend the cashews & soaking liquid until smooth in a blender. Combine 1 & 3/4 cups of potato flakes or 1/2 cup of the potato flour with the wheat and 1/4 tsp. of salt in a bowl. Stir in the cashew paste until dough forms.

- To make the filling, mix the next 6 ingredients with 1/4 cup of water in a saucepan. Bring to a boil, then moderately lower heat. Stirring periodically, heat the sweet potato for approximately 5 minutes until it is halfway done. Add the kale after stirring. When the sweet potato is ready, uncover and simmer for a further 5 minutes, adding water and 1-2 tbsp. At a time, as necessary, to avoid sticking.

- Add the remaining 1/2 cup of potato flakes or 3 tablespoons of potato flour, nutritional yeast, milk, and vinegar to a blender; until smooth, blend. Add the remaining 1/4 tsp. Salt, the milk mixture, and the crushed red pepper to the veggies. To taste and season as necessary.

- For 15 minutes, preheat the air fryer to 175°C. Four 8 by 11-inch pieces of parchment paper should be cut out. Add whole wheat flour and sift it onto a clean board. Four parts of dough should be formed into balls. Roll 1 ball into a circle (8-inch) on a floured surface. Leave a 1-inch margin after spooning 1/2 cup of filling into the circle's bottom half. To create a half-moon, fold the empty half over the filled half. With a fork, seal the edge, then brush more milk on top.

- Dust one piece of parchment with flour. On parchment, place the calzone. Place paper in air fryer by lifting by the edges for 8 minutes or till the top is browned in the air fryer.

- Repeat the process with the rest of the dough balls & filling. Serve marinara sauce with the calzones.

Nutritional values per serving:

Total Calories: 400kcal, Fats: 12g, Carbohydrates: 60g, Protein: 6g

26. Air Fried Mixed Veggies
Ready in: 45 mins.

Serves: 4

Difficulty: easy

Ingredients:

- 6-8 cauliflower florets (medium)
- 1 tbsp. of oil
- ½ green bell pepper (medium), cubed
- 1 carrot (medium), chopped
- ½ red bell pepper (medium) cubed
- ¼ cup of peas
- 1 potato (medium), chopped

Spices:

- 3 tbsp. of curry paste
- 1 tbsp. of oil
- 1 tbsp. of coriander powder
- 1 tsp. of red chilli powder or paprika, or to taste

- ¼ tsp. of turmeric powder
- 1 tbsp. of garam masala powder
- salt to taste

Directions:

- Combine chopped carrots, cauliflower florets, and potatoes in a mixing basin with the oil.
- For 10 minutes, preheat your air fryer at 180°C.
- With 1 tablespoon oil, toss the vegetables (chopped carrots, cauliflower, and potatoes) and air fry for 7 minutes.
- Combine the curry paste, oil, and all the spices—turmeric, paprika or red chilli powder, garam masala powder, and coriander powder—in a separate bowl.
- Blend them well.
- Place the peas, along with the green and red peppers, in a bowl.
- Pour the spice blend into a mixing dish.
- The semi-fried veggies (potato, cauliflower, and carrots) should now be added to the mixing bowl.
- With a spoon, combine everything to evenly distribute the spice mixture over each veggie.
- Reload the basket of air fryer with the hot veggies.
- At 180°C, air fried all the veggies for 10 minutes.
- Provide hot with bread or rice.

Nutritional values per serving:

Total Calories: 110kcal, Fats: 4g, Carbohydrates: 38g, Protein: 14g

27. Stuffed Eggplant
Ready in: 20 mins.

Serves: 4

Difficulty: medium

Ingredients:

- 2 tsp. of Oil divided

- 8 Baby Eggplants, rinse & pat dry
- 1 tbsp. of Cilantro leaves for garnishing

Spice Stuffing:

- 1 tsp. of Ground Cumin
- ¾ tbsp. of Coriander powder
- ½ tsp. of Red Chili powder
- ½ tsp. of Garlic powder
- ½ tsp. of Ground Turmeric
- 1 tsp. of Salt
- ¾ tbsp. of Dry Mango powder

Directions:

- Combine the stuffing spices in a bowl.
- Take the eggplants & keep the stems whole. Slit the middle of each eggplant, starting at the bottom and continuing up to just above stem. It should not break into two parts when you cut it. The eggplant should now be turned 90 degrees, and a new incision should be cut from the middle. Cut the eggplant in half lengthwise while retaining the stem.
- You may also add a tsp. of oil to the spice mixture. Fill each of the eggplants' slits with spices using a small spoon or knife.
- Arrange the eggplants in the Air Fryer in a single layer. Oil each eggplant by brushing it. Brush oil on opposite side as you turn around.
- Turn on the air fryer and wait 8 to 12 minutes at 180°C. When they are cooked, their colour will change. At 8 minutes, check, and cook for longer if necessary. At roughly six minutes, you may flip them around, although it is not required.
- Enjoy with cilantro as a garnish!

Nutritional values per serving:

Total Calories: 106 kcal, Fats: 3g, Carbohydrates: 20g, Protein: 3g

28. Stuffed Bitter Gourd
Ready in: 50 mins.

Serves: 6

Difficulty: medium

Ingredients:

- 3 sliced onions
- 12 bitter gourds, small
- 1 tbsp. of ginger garlic paste
- 1 tbsp. of coriander powder
- 1 tsp. of cumin powder
- 1 tsp. of aniseed powder
- 1 tsp. of cayenne
- ½ tsp. of garam masala
- 1 tsp. of tamarind paste
- 1/2 tsp. of fenugreek seeds
- salt to taste
- Mustard oil for frying

Directions:

- Use a knife to delicately scrape the bitter gourd.
- Cut a vertical split through the bitter gourd from top to bottom, and then scoop out the meat and seeds.
- Throw away the seeds. Apply some salt to the interior and exterior of the bitter gourd to lessen its bitterness, and then set it aside for 30 minutes.
- After 30 minutes, rinse the bitter gourd to remove all of the salt, dry it, and set it away. To mildly cook the bitter gourd, either microwave it for two minutes or parboil it for two to three minutes with a little tamarind paste (approximately one-fourth teaspoon).

Prepare the stuffing:

- In a pan, add 1 teaspoon of mustard oil. Add the minced ginger and garlic and cook till golden brown. When it has cooled, mix into a thick paste. Cook for a further period of time after adding salt and all the spice powders. Make the stuffing substantial. Examine the flavour and adjust the spice. Allow the filling to cool totally.

Get the bitter gourd ready:

- Take the bitter gourd that has been split open now, and liberally pour the filling inside. To keep them intact, wrap the regular sewing thread around them.
- Preheat the air fryer for five minutes at 200°C. On the basket of the air fryer, spray or brush oil.
- Place the basket with the stuffed bitter gourd in it and air fried for 6 to 8 minutes, or until the bitter gourd is golden brown and just beginning to crisp up. Continue to check every 3 to 4 minutes. Remove them, then serve them hot with bread.

Nutritional values per serving:

Total Calories: 73 kcal, Fats: 1g, Carbohydrates: 15g, Protein: 3g

29. Pumpkin Pie

Ready in: 30 mins.

Serves: 5

Difficulty: medium

Ingredients:

- ½ cup of granulated sugar
- 1 can (15 ounces) of pure pumpkin
- ½ cup of brown sugar
- ½ tsp. of ground ginger
- 1 tsp. of ground cinnamon
- ½ tsp. of ground nutmeg
- ½ cup of heavy cream or milk
- 2 eggs (large)
- ½ cup of evaporated milk (not condensed sweetened milk)
- 1 pie crust

Directions:

- Roll the pie dough into the pie pan to prepare it for baking. Place the pie's shell in the basket of the air fryer and cook for approximately 5 minutes at 175°C. In contrast, making the filling, set it aside.

- To make the filling, combine the sugar, pumpkin puree, brown sugar, ginger, cinnamon, and nutmeg in a mixing bowl. Continue blending while remaining together.

- Add the eggs and combine everything with a whisk. Milk and evaporated milk should be added gradually. Once the filling is combined, smooth, and creamy, continue stirring.

- Gently pour the prepped pie crust with the filling of pumpkin pie within. Place the pie into the air fryer for a further 25 to 30 minutes, or until the middle is no longer wobbly. You may have to add an extra two to three minutes.

Nutritional values per serving:

Total Calories: 353 kcal, **Fats:** 12g, **Carbohydrates:** 58g, **Protein:** 7g

Chapter 9: Air Fried Diabetic Diet ~ Snack Recipes

1. Coconut Crusted Air Fried Turkey Fingers

Ready in: 30 mins.

Serves: 6

Difficulty: easy

Ingredients:

- 2 tsp. of sesame oil
- 2 egg whites (large)
- 1/2 cup of shredded coconut (sweetened), lightly toasted
- 2 tbsp. of sesame seeds, toasted
- 1/2 cup of dry bread crumbs
- 1/2 tsp. of salt
- Cooking spray
- 1~1/2 pounds of turkey breast tenderloins in half~inch strips

Dipping sauce:

- 1/3 cup of pineapple juice, unsweetened
- 1/2 cup of plum sauce
- 1 tsp. of cornstarch
- 1~1/2 tsp. of prepared mustard
- Optional: lime wedges and Grated lime zest

Directions:

- Set the air fryer up to 205°C. Whisk the egg whites & oil together in a small bowl. Combine coconut, sesame seeds, bread crumbs, and salt in a separate shallow dish. To help the coating stick, pat the turkey after dipping it in the egg mixture and the coconut mixture.

- Working in batches, arrange the turkey in the air-fryer basket on the oiled tray in a single layer. Mist with cooking spray. Cook for 3 to 4 minutes or until golden brown. Toss with cooking spray and turn. Cook for a further 3–4 minutes or until

the turkey is golden brown and no longer pink.

- Meanwhile, combine the sauce's components in a small pot. Bring to boil; simmer and stir for 1~2 minutes or until thickened. Serve sauce with the turkey. Serve turkey strips with lime wedges and, at your discretion, lime zest on top.

Nutritional values per serving:

Total Calories: 292 kcal, **Fats:** 9 g, **Carbohydrates:** 24 g, **Protein:** 31 g

2. Turkey Croquettes

Ready in: 30 mins.

Serves: 6

Difficulty: easy

Ingredients:

- 1/2 cup of grated Parmesan cheese
- 2 cups of mashed potatoes (with added butter and milk)
- 1/2 cup of Swiss cheese, shredded
- 2 tsp. of fresh rosemary (minced), or 1/2 tsp. of rosemary (dried), crushed
- 1 finely chopped shallot
- 1 tsp. of fresh sage, minced or 1/4 tsp. of sage leaves, dried
- 1/4 tsp. of pepper
- 1/2 tsp. of salt
- 3 cups of cooked turkey, finely chopped
- 2 tbsp. of water
- 1 egg (large)
- 1~1/4 cups of panko bread crumbs
- Sour cream (optional)
- Cooking spray, Butter-flavored

Directions:

- Set air fryer up to 175°C. Mash potatoes with cheeses, rosemary, shallot, sage, salt, & pepper in a large bowl; mix in turkey. Lightly but thoroughly combine. Form into twelve patties that are 1 inch thick.

- Eggs and water should be whisked in a small bowl. Another small bowl should be filled with bread crumbs. Croquettes should be dipped in a mixture of egg, then coated with bread crumbs by patting them down.
- Working in batches, arrange the croquettes in one single layer on the prepared baking sheet within the air-fryer basket. Cook for 4-5 minutes, or until golden brown. Toss with cooking spray and turn. Cook for 4-5 minutes, or until golden brown. Serve with sour cream, if preferred.

Nutritional values per serving:

Total Calories: 322 kcal, **Fats:** 12 g, Carbohydrates: 22g, **Protein:** 29 g

3. Fish & Chips
Ready in: 35 mins.

Serves: 2

Difficulty: medium

Ingredients:

- 1 tbsp. of olive oil
- 1 potato (medium)
- 1/8 tsp. of salt
- 1/8 tsp. of pepper

For Fish:

- 1/8 tsp. of pepper
- 3 tbsp. of all-purpose flour
- 1 egg (large)
- 1/3 cup of crushed cornflakes
- 2 tbsp. of water
- 1-1/2 tsp. of grated Parmesan cheese
- 1/8 tsp. of salt
- Dash of cayenne pepper
- 1/2 pound of cod or haddock fillets
- Tartar sauce (optional)

Directions:

- Set the air fryer up to 205°C. Potatoes should be peeled and cut into 1/2-in. Slices should be thick and sliced into 1/2-in. -heavy sticks.
- Toss the potato with the oil, pepper, and salt in a large bowl. Place the potato pieces in the air fryer basket in a single layer, and cook for 5 to 10 minutes, or until just soft. Re-distribute the potatoes in the basket and cook for a further 5–10 minutes, or until they are crisp and lightly browned.
- Meanwhile, combine the flour and pepper in a small bowl. Whisk egg and water in a separate shallow bowl. Mix cornflakes, cheese, and cayenne in a third bowl. After salting the fish, cover both sides with the flour mixture, and brush off the excess. After dipping in the egg mixture, massage the coated object to help the coating stick.
- Take out the fries and keep them heated. Put the fish in the air fryer basket in a single layer. Cook for 8 to 10 minutes, flipping once until the fish is gently browned and just starting to easily flakes with a fork. Avoid overcooking. Heat up the fries in the basket once more. Serve right away. Serve with tartar sauce, if preferred.

Nutritional values per serving:

Total Calories: 304 kcal, **Fats:** 9 g, **Carbohydrates:** 33 g, **Protein:** 23 g

4. Crusted Sweet Potato Chicken Nuggets
Ready in: 25 mins.

Serves: 4

Difficulty: easy

Ingredients:

- 1/4 cup of all-purpose flour
- 1 cup of sweet potato chips
- 1 tsp. of salt, divided
- 1/4 tsp. of baking powder
- 1/2 tsp. of pepper, coarsely ground

- 1 tbsp. of cornstarch
- Cooking spray
- 1 pound of chicken tenderloins, in 1-1/2" pieces

Directions:

- Set air fryer up to 205°C. Grind the chips, flour, pepper, baking powder, and 1/2 tsp. Salt in a food processor. Place on a small plate.
- Toss the chicken with the cornstarch mixture and the rest of 1/2 tsp. Salt. Combine potato chip mixture with chicken and toss to coat.
- Place the chicken, in batches, in one single layer on the oiled pan within the air fryer basket. Spray with cooking spray. Cook for 3 to 4 minutes or until golden brown. Toss with cooking spray and turn. Cook for a further 3–4 minutes or until the chicken is golden brown and no longer pink.

Nutritional values per serving:

Total Calories: 190 kcal, Fats: 4 g, Carbohydrates: 13g, Protein: 28 g

5. Potato Chips
Ready in: 35 mins.

Serves: 6

Difficulty: easy

Ingredients:

- Olive oil cooking spray
- 2 potatoes (large)
- Fresh parsley (Minced), optional
- 1/2 tsp. of sea salt

Directions:

- Set the air fryer up to 175°C. Slice potatoes into extremely tiny pieces using a vegetable peeler or mandoline. Transfer to a big basin and cover with cold water. Drain after a 15-minute soak. 15 additional minutes of soaking after adding more cold water.

- Potatoes should be drained, placed on towels, and dried. Potatoes should be sprayed with cooking spray and salt. Put potato slices in one single layer on the oiled tray in the air fryer basket in batches. Cook for 15–17 minutes, tossing and rotating every 5-7 minutes, until crisp & golden brown. Add some parsley, if desired.

Nutritional values per serving:

Total Calories: 148 kcal, Fats: 1 g, Carbohydrates: 32g, Protein: 4 g

6. Cauliflower Gnocchi & Marinara Sauce
Ready in: 20 mins.

Serves: 8

Difficulty: medium

Ingredients:

- 3 tbsp. of extra-virgin olive oil, divided
- 2 packages of cauliflower gnocchi, frozen (10 ounces), thawed & divided
- ½ cup of Parmesan cheese (grated), divided
- 1 cup of marinara sauce (reduced-sodium), warmed
- 2 tbsp. of chopped flat-leaf parsley, fresh

Directions:

- Set the air fryer up to 190°C. In a big bowl, combine 1 package of gnocchi, 1 1/2 teaspoons of oil, and 2 tablespoons of Parmesan.
- Spray cooking spray on the air fryer's basket. Once in the basket, add the gnocchi mixture and cook for 5 minutes, flipping once. Transfer to a big bowl. The remaining gnocchi, oil, and tbsp. Parmesan should be used in a similar manner. The rest of 1/4 cup of Parmesan and the parsley should be added to the cooked gnocchi. Serve alongside marinara.

Nutritional values per serving:

Total Calories: 160 kcal, Fats: 9 g, Carbohydrates: 14 g, Protein: 3g

7. Bacon Wrapped Scallops

Ready in: 20 mins.

Serves: 6

Difficulty: medium

Ingredients:

- 3 thin bacon slices, center-cut
- 12 sea scallops, medium (about almost 9 ounces total)
- ¼ tsp. of ground pepper
- 1 tsp. of olive oil
- ¼ tsp. of paprika

Directions:

- Set the air fryer up to 190°C. Pat the scallops dry. Each scallop's side muscle should be removed and discarded. To create 12 strips of bacon, cut each piece in half lengthwise and then across. Wrap 1 strip of bacon around each scallop, gently overlapping the ends. To hold the bacon in place, put one wooden pick through the other side of the scallop and through both of the bacon ends. Along with a little oil brush, evenly distribute the pepper and paprika over the scallops.
- Place the scallops into the fryer basket in an equal layer. Cook for 10 to 12 minutes, or till the bacon is starting to crisp & the scallops get firm yet soft.

Nutritional values per serving:

Total Calories: 43 kcal, **Fats:** 2 g, **Carbohydrates:** 1 g, **Protein:** 5 g

8. Feta Beets

Ready in: 30 mins.

Serves: 4

Difficulty: easy

Ingredients:

- 1 tbsp. of olive oil
- 1 pound of beets (3 small or 2 large), trimmed & peeled, cut in one-inch pieces
- ¼ tsp. of salt
- ¼ cup of feta cheese, crumbled
- ¼ tsp. of ground pepper
- 1 tbsp. of chopped fresh oregano

Directions:

- Set the air fryer up to 205°C and wait five minutes. Beets should be placed in a large bowl with oil, salt, and pepper. Toss to coat.
- Place the beets into the fryer basket in a single layer, and cook for 8-10 minutes. Be careful while flipping the beets, and cook for 6 to 8 minutes, or until the edges are caramelized and crispy. Add feta and oregano to the serving plate after transfer.

Nutritional values per serving:

Total Calories: 106 kcal, **Fats:** 6 g, **Carbohydrates:** 12g, **Protein:** 3 g

9. Cinnamon Apples

Ready in: 10 mins.

Serves: 2

Difficulty: easy

Ingredients:

- 1 tsp. of Ground Cinnamon
- 2 Apples (Large)
- 1/8 tsp. of Salt

Directions:

- Set air fryer up to 198°C.
- In a mixing dish, combine sugar and cinnamon.
- Each apple should be cut into eighths.
- Combine the sugar and cinnamon with the apples.
- Arrange the apple wedges into the air fryer in a single layer.
- Do 4 minutes of cooking at 198°C.
- After flipping, sauté the apple wedges for a further 4 minutes, or until they are crisp.
- The apple wedges should be placed on a wire rack to cool fully.

- Continue frying apple wedges in single layers until they are all done and cooled.
- Consume immediately or keep in an airtight container.

Nutritional values per serving:

Total Calories: 50 kcal, **Fats:** 2 g, **Carbohydrates:** 15 g, **Protein:** 4 g

10. Zucchini Fries

Ready in: 30 mins.

Serves: 6

Difficulty: medium

Ingredients:

For Zucchini Fries:

- ½ cup of almond flour
- 2 Zucchinis, cut in fries (medium)
- ¼ cup of pork rinds (ground), plain
- 1 tsp. of garlic sea salt
- ¼ cup of parmesan cheese, grated
- 1 tsp. of dried parsley
- ½ tsp. of oregano
- 1 tsp. of dried basil
- 2 beaten eggs

For sauce:

- 2 tsp. of prepared horseradish
- ½ cup of mayonnaise
- 2 tbsp. of ketchup (without sugar)
- 1 tsp. of garlic salt
- 1 tsp. of smoked paprika
- ½ tsp. of fresh lemon juice

Directions:

- Set a regular oven to 205°C if you're baking them in an air fryer.
- Establish the breading station. In a bowl, combine the almond flour, pork rinds, cheese, basil, parsley, oregano, and garlic salt. Eggs should be combined in a separate bowl.

- After dipping the zucchini in the egg, coat it with the breading (lightly, don't press in the mixture). Shake off any extra breading before placing the food onto a baking rack coated with parchment or Silpat) that has been sprayed with olive oil.
- After all of the breaded zucchini are placed on the baking trays, coat the tops with the olive oil spray & bake at 205°C for 15 to 20 minutes, or till golden brown. About halfway through cooking, rotate or switch the pans.
- Make the dipping sauce while zucchini fries are baking. In a bowl, mix and whisk all the sauce components until well incorporated.
- Before serving, give the zucchini fries a little time to cool.

Nutritional values per serving:

Total Calories: 257 kcal, **Fats:** 22 g, Carbohydrates: 5 g, **Protein:** 8 g

11. Chicken Wings

Ready in: 55 mins.

Serves: 10

Difficulty: medium

Ingredients:

- 1 pound of Chicken Wings
- 2 tbsp. of Berbere
- 2 tbsp. of Olive Oil
- 1 tsp. of garlic powder
- Salt & pepper to taste

Directions:

- Combine the olive oil, chicken wings, salt, garlic powder, and Berbere in a zip lock bag.
- Overnight marinating gives them more taste, but 30 minutes will suffice if you want them right away.
- Spray some olive oil on the air fryer tray (or pam). As a result, the wings won't adhere to the tray.

- In accordance with the manufacturer's instructions, air fry them.
- Serve and savour!

Nutritional values per serving:

Total Calories: 420 kcal, **Fats:** 20 g, Carbohydrates: 0 g, **Protein:** 60 g

12. Bolognese Zucchini Boats
Ready in: 27 mins.

Serves: 4

Difficulty: medium

Ingredients:

- 2 Zucchinis (Medium)
- 300 g of Pork Mince
- ½ Diced Onion (Large)
- 400 g of Tinned Tomatoes
- 1 Tbsp. of Garlic Puree
- 2 Tsp. of Oregano
- 50 g of Hard Cheese, optional
- Salt & black Pepper

Directions:

- Fill the cake pan of air fryer with your garlic, minced pork, sliced onion, salt, and pepper. In the air fryer, cook for 8 mins at 180°C.
- Add the oregano and canned tomatoes, and simmer for 2 minutes further at 200°C.
- Cut the zucchini lengthwise in half, then use a spoon to scoop out the centre.
- When air fryer beeps, fill the zucchini boats with the cooked Bolognese and set them on the grill pan in the air fryer. Cook at 180°C for 10 minutes further.
- After the beep, top with cheese and cook for an additional 2 minutes at 200°C.

Nutritional values per serving:

Total Calories: 309 kcal, **Fats:** 21 g, Carbohydrates: 13 g, **Protein:** 19 g

13. Onion Rings
Ready in: 25 mins.

Serves: 5

Difficulty: medium

Ingredients:

- 1 & ¼ cup of Flour
- 1 Onion, Sliced
- 1 tsp. of Baking Powder
- 1 cup + 1 tsp. of Milk
- 1 Beaten Egg
- ¾ cup of Bread Crumbs Seasonings

Directions:

- Set your air fryer up to 185°C and prepare a nonstick basket.
- Combine the flour, baking powder, and spices in a mixing dish.
- Add the egg and milk after combining (or beer). Move into a small dish.
- Your bread crumbs should be placed in a small basin. Take the 1st slice of onion and, using a fork, thoroughly dredge it in the ingredients from the first bowl.
- Next, coat this piece with bread crumbs. After that, put it in the basket. Repeat this with the remaining slices, being careful not to overlap them too much.
- After 8 minutes, turn the onion rings over in the air fryer. Continue air frying for a further 8 minutes.

Nutritional values per serving:

Total Calories: 172 kcal, **Fats:** 4 g, **Carbohydrates:** 15 g, **Protein:** 11 g

14. Crab Rangoon
Ready in: 30 mins.

Serves: 8

Difficulty: medium

Ingredients:

- 2 ounces of cream cheese at room temp
- 2 ounces of imitation crab meat
- 1½ tbsp. of chopped green onions, small
- 16 wonton wrappers
- ½ tbsp. of Worcestershire sauce
- oil for spritzing

Directions:

- In a small bowl, combine the cream cheese, green onions, crab meat, and Worcestershire sauce.
- For 10 minutes, preheat the air fryer on broil while the basket of air frying is inside.
- Begin folding your crab Rangoon while the air fryer is heating up. On a cooling rack, arrange eight wonton wrappers. They won't get too wet because of this. Each wonton should have 1 1/2 tbsp. of filling in the middle. Apply a little amount of water just outside the corner filings. Fold into the shape.
- Spray some oil on the basket. 8 crab Rangoon should be placed in the basket. Set the temperature to 149°C. Air fry for 4-5 minutes. Each one should be turned over and given another oil spritz. 3-5 more minutes, or till golden brown.
- Take out and let cool until you're ready to serve on the cooling rack. Continue with the second batch. Enjoy! Serve with your preferred dipping sauce!

Nutritional values per serving:

Total Calories: 76 kcal, **Fats:** 3 g, **Carbohydrates:** 11g, **Protein:** 2 g

15. Air Fried Churros
Ready in: 20 mins.

Serves: 4

Difficulty: medium

Ingredients:

- 1/3 cup of butter (unsalted), cut into cubes
- 1 cup of water
- 2 Tbsp. of granulated sugar
- 1 cup of all-purpose flour
- 1/4 tsp. of salt
- 2 eggs (large)
- oil spray
- 1 tsp. of vanilla extract

Sugar cinnamon coating:

- 3/4 tsp. of ground cinnamon
- 1/2 cup of granulated sugar

Directions:

- Place an oil spray-coated baking sheet on top of a silicone baking mat.
- Combine water, sugar, butter, and salt in a medium pot. Heat to a rolling boil over medium-high.
- Flour is added to the pot when the heat is reduced to medium-low. Cook while regularly mixing the dough using a rubber spatula until it comes together & is smooth.
- Remove the dough from the heat and place it in a mixing bowl. Allow cooling for four minutes.
- Use a stand mixer or electric hand mixer to combine the dough by adding the eggs & vanilla extract into the mixing bowl. It will resemble sticky mashed potatoes. Put lumps in a ball with your hands & transfer them to a big piping bag with a huge star-shaped tip.
- Use a pastry bag to pipe churros into 4-inch lengths, then trim the ends with scissors.
- On the baking sheet, chill the piped churros for an hour.
- Carefully transfer the churros to the basket of Air Fryer using a cookie spatula, allowing a gap of approximately 1/2 inch

between each one. Churros should be sprayed with oil. The size of the air fryer will determine how many batches you need to cook them.

- Air fry until golden brown for 10 to 12 minutes at 190°C.

- Combine cinnamon and granulated sugar in a small basin.

- As soon as the churros are done baking, put them in to bowl with the mixture of sugar & toss to coat. Doing so in groups. Serve hot with chocolate or Nutella dipping sauce.

Nutritional values per serving:

Total Calories: 204 kcal, Fats: 9 g, Carbohydrates: 27 g, Protein: 3 g

16. Egg Rolls
Ready in: 46 mins.

Serves: 12

Difficulty: medium

Ingredients:

- 1/2 onion

- 1/2 pound of ground pork

- 1/2 bag of coleslaw mix

- 1 stalk of celery

- 4 ounces of mushrooms

- 12 wrappers of egg roll

- 1/2 tsp. of salt

Directions:

- A skillet should be heated to medium.

- Cook the onion and ground pork together until the meat loses its pink colour.

- Season the pan with salt and add the celery, mushrooms, and coleslaw mixture. The veggies should cook for 5 mins to soften.

- Place the package on the cutting board. To the upper corner of the egg roll wrapper, add 1/3 cup of the filling ingredients. Over the filling, fold the top down. After that, roll up the wrapper

while tucking the edges in. When you reach the bottom, wet the wrapper's edges with your fingertips to secure it in place.

- Keep rolling the egg rolls till all of the fillings have been used.

- If desired, gently mist the egg rolls with cooking spray. The egg rolls will be evenly browned as a result.

- Cook egg rolls for 6 to 8 minutes at 205°C, turning them over with tongs once halfway through.

Nutritional values per serving:

Total Calories: 76 kcal, Fats: 5g, Carbohydrates: 3g, Protein: 5 g

17. Stuffed Mushrooms
Ready in: 18 mins.

Serves: 12

Difficulty: easy

Ingredients:

- 6 oz. of softened Cream Cheese

- 16 oz. of White Button Mushrooms (Whole)

- 3 tbsp. of Sour Cream

- ½ tsp. of Garlic Powder

- ¼ cup of Cheddar Cheese, Shredded

- ½ tsp. of Salt

- Chives (Chopped) for topping

- Dash of black Pepper

- Oil Spray

Directions:

- Clean off any dirt or debris from the mushrooms using a moist paper towel (they can get slimy if rinsed underwater.) Trim or remove the mushroom stems.

- Cream cheese, garlic powder, sour cream, salt, & pepper should all be combined in a bowl. The mixture should be placed into each mushroom cap's "well." Add chives and cheddar cheese shavings to the top of each.

- Oil spray the air fryer basket to stop it from sticking. In the basket, arrange the mushrooms in a single layer. Cook for 8–10 minutes at a temperature of 185°C. Prior to serving, let it cool somewhat.

Nutritional values per serving:

Total Calories: 86 kcal, Fats: 2g, Carbohydrates: 3g, Protein: 2 g

18. Pretzel Bites
Ready in: 21 mins.

Serves: 30

Difficulty: medium

Ingredients:

- 2 & 1/4 tsp. of quick rise yeast
- 1 1/2 cups of water
- 4 cups of all-purpose flour
- 1 tbsp. of sugar/honey
- 1 tsp. of sea salt
- 4 cups of water
- 1/3 cup of baking soda
- 1 beaten egg
- 1 tbsp. of water
- 3 tbsp. of melted butter

Optional:

- Baking Soda Bath
- Pretzel salt
- Egg Wash
- Butter topping

Directions:

Prepare the Dough:

- Water and yeast should be combined in a mixing bowl. Stir.
- Stir in the sea salt, sugar, & flour until largely incorporated.
- Lightly dust your hands and use your hands to knead the dough for 1 minute, forming a ball. The dough should be divided into eighths.

- Form dough ropes on a surface that has been gently dusted with flour.
- Cut the dough into pieces that are 1 inch long using a floured knife.
- Lightly olive oil brush the air fryer's basket. Give the pretzel bits space to expand as you add them to the basket.
- Cook for 5-6 minutes at 198°C, or until the top is just beginning to brown. Brush heated pretzel bits with melted butter and pretzel salt if you're using the butter technique.

Nutritional values per serving:

Total Calories: 37 kcal, Fats: 1g, Carbohydrates: 8g, Protein: 1g

19. Pretzel Dogs
Ready in: 27 mins.

Serves: 8

Difficulty: medium

Ingredients:

- 1/2 cup of warm water
- 8 hot dogs
- 3/4 tsp. of quick rise yeast
- 1/4 tsp. of sea salt
- 1 1/3 cup of all-purpose flour, and some more for dusting}
- 1/4 tsp. of sugar
- pretzel salt, optional
- 2 tbsp. of melted butter
- olive oil
- sesame seeds, optional

Directions:

- Water and yeast should be combined in a mixing bowl. Stir in the sugar, flour, and sea salt until mostly incorporated.

- Using a little flour, knead the dough using your hand for a minute, forming a ball as you go. The dough should be divided into eighths.

- Based on the size of the hot dog, shape the dough into ropes that are 14 to 20 inches long on a lightly dusted surface.

- Roll the dough as you wrap it around the hot dog, starting at 1 of the ends. To keep the dough pieces together, gently squeeze each end.

- Olive oil should be brushed over the air fryer's basket. Put the pretzel dogs in the basket, allowing them to expand slightly.

- Cook for 7 mins at 198°C, or until the top is just beginning to brown. Pretzel salt or sesame seeds may be added after brushing heated pretzel bits with melted butter.

Nutritional values per serving:

Total Calories: 213 kcal, **Fats:** 10g, Carbohydrates: 24 g, Protein: 7g

20. Air-Fried Ravioli

Ready in: 30 mins.

Serves: 6

Difficulty: easy

Ingredients:

- 1/4 cup of Parmesan cheese, shredded

- 1 cup of bread crumbs, seasoned

- 2 tsp. of dried basil

- 2 eggs (large), lightly beaten

- 1/2 cup of all-purpose flour

- 1 package of frozen beef ravioli (9 ounces), thawed

- Fresh basil (minced), optional

- Cooking spray

- 1 cup of marinara sauce, warmed

Directions:

- Set the air fryer up to 170°C. Combine basil, Parmesan cheese, and bread crumbs in a small bowl. Put the flour and

the eggs in separate, small dishes. Shake off excess flour after coating the ravioli on both sides. In order to make the coating adhere, dip in the eggs, then into the crumb mixture.

- Ravioli should be arranged in one single layer on a greased tray in the air fryer basket and sprayed with cooking spray in batches. Cook for 3 to 4 minutes or until golden brown. Toss with cooking spray and turn. Cook for 3–4 more minutes, or until golden brown. Sprinkle basil and extra Parmesan cheese right away, if preferred. With marinara sauce, serve warm.

Nutritional values per serving:

Total Calories: 40kcal, **Fats:** 1g, **Carbohydrates:** 6g, **Proteins:** 2g

21. Cheeseburger Onion Rings

Ready in: 40 mins.

Serves: 8

Difficulty: medium

Ingredients:

- 1/3 cup of ketchup

- 1 pound of ground beef, lean (90% lean)

- 2 tbsp. of prepared mustard

- 1 onion (large)

- 1/2 tsp. of salt

- 4 ounces of cheddar cheese in 8 squares

- 2 tsp. of garlic powder

- 3/4 cup of all-purpose flour

- 2 eggs (large), lightly beaten

- Cooking spray

- 1-1/2 cups of panko bread crumbs

- Ketchup, optional

Directions:

- Set the air fryer at 160°C. Beef, ketchup, mustard, and salt are combined in a small bowl while being softly but completely mixed. Slice onion into 1/2-inch rings after cutting it. Place half of the meat mixture into 8 slices (save other onion rings for one other use). Add the square of cheese & the leftover meat mixture to each.

- Mix flour & garlic powder in a small bowl. Put eggs in one shallow dish, followed by bread crumbs. Shake off excess flour after dipping stuffed onion rings in it to cover both sides. To help the coating stick, dip in the egg, then coat in the bread crumbs

- On a greased tray in the air fryer basket, arrange onion rings in one single layer in batches and spritz with the cooking spray. Cook for 12 to 15 minutes, or until the beef thermometer reaches 80°C and the surface is golden brown. Serve with spicy ketchup, if preferred.

Nutritional values per serving:

Total Calories: 258kcal, Fats: 11g, Carbohydrates: 19g, Proteins: 19g

22. Sriracha Crispy Spring Rolls
Ready in: 1 hr.

Serves: 24

Difficulty: medium

Ingredients:

- 3 chopped green onions

- 3 cups of coleslaw mix (almost about 7 ounces)

- 1 tbsp. of soy sauce

- 1 pound of skinless, boneless chicken breasts

- 1 tsp. of sesame oil

- 1 tsp. of seasoned salt

- 2 tbsp. of Sriracha chilli sauce

- 2 packages of cream cheese (8 ounces each), softened

- 24 wrappers of spring roll

- Optional: more green onions and Sweet chilli sauce

- Cooking spray

Directions:

- Set the air fryer up to 178°C. As the chicken cooks, combine the coleslaw mix, soy sauce, green onions, and sesame oil. Put the chicken in the air fryer basket in one single layer on an oiled tray. Cook for 18–20 minutes, or until a thermometer placed in the chicken registers 80°C. Remove chicken, and let it cool. Chicken should be chopped finely and then salted.

- Heat the air fryer to 205°C. Cream cheese & Sriracha chilli sauce should be combined in a big bowl before adding the chicken and coleslaw combination. Put roughly 2 teaspoons of filling directly below the wrapper's centre, with one corner facing you. (Until ready to use, cover the leftover wrappers with a wet paper towel.) Fold the bottom corner over the filling and wet the other corners. Over the filling, fold the side corners toward the centre. Roll firmly, pushing the tip to seal. Repeat.

- Spring rolls should be arranged in one single layer on a greased tray in the air fryer basket and sprayed with cooking spray in batches. Cook for 5 to 6 minutes, until gently browned. Toss with cooking spray and turn. Cook for a further 5 to 6 minutes, or until crisp and golden. Serve with green onions and sweet chilli sauce, if preferred.

Nutritional values per serving:

Total Calories: 127kcal, Fats: 7g, Carbohydrates: 10g, Proteins: 6g

23. Air-Fried Calamari
Ready in: 30 mins.

Serves: 5

Difficulty: medium

Ingredients:

- 1/2 tsp. of salt

- 1/2 cup of all-purpose flour

- 1 egg (large), lightly beaten

- 1 cup of panko bread crumbs

- 1/2 cup of 2% milk

- 1/2 tsp. of seasoned salt
- 8 ounces of cleaned, frozen or fresh calamari, thawed & cut into half-inch rings
- 1/4 tsp. of pepper
- Cooking spray

Directions:

- Set the air fryer up to 205°C. Flour and salt should be combined in a small bowl. Whisk the egg and milk in a separate shallow dish. Combine bread crumbs, seasoning salt, and pepper in a third small bowl. Calamari should be covered in a flour mixture, then dipped in egg mixture and bread crumbs combination.
- Calamari should be placed in single layers on a greased tray in the air fryer basket and sprayed with cooking spray in batches. 4 minutes to cook. Toss with cooking spray and turn. Cook for 3-5 more minutes, or until golden brown.

Nutritional values per serving:

Total Calories: 11kcal, **Fats:** 0g, **Carbohydrates:** 1g, **Proteins:** 1g

24. Mushroom Roll-Ups
Ready in: 40 mins.

Serves: 10

Difficulty: easy

Ingredients:

- 8 ounces of Portobello mushrooms (large), finely chopped & gills discarded
- 2 tbsp. of olive oil
- 1 tsp. of dried oregano
- 1/2 tsp. of crushed red pepper flakes
- 1 tsp. of dried thyme
- 1/4 tsp. of salt
- 4 ounces of ricotta cheese, whole-milk
- 1 package of cream cheese (8 ounces), softened
- 10 (8 inches) flour tortillas

- Mint sauce
- Cooking spray

Directions:

- Heat oil in a skillet over medium heat. Add the mushrooms and cook for 4 minutes. Add salt, pepper flakes, oregano, and thyme. Sauté for 4-6 minutes, or until mushrooms are browned. Cool.
- Combine the cheeses, then thoroughly fold in the mushrooms. Place 3 tablespoons of the mushroom mixture in the middle of each tortilla's bottom. Roll firmly, then use toothpicks to fasten.
- Set the air fryer up to 205°C. Place roll-ups in the air fryer basket in batches on a greased tray and spritz with the cooking spray. Cook for 9 to 11 minutes or until golden brown. Discard toothpicks after roll-ups have cooled enough to handle. Eat with mint sauce.

Nutritional values per serving:

Total Calories: 291kcal, **Fats:** 16g, Carbohydrates: 31g, **Proteins:** 8g

25. Garlic Bread
Ready in: 20 mins.

Serves: 8

Difficulty: easy

Ingredients:

- 3 tbsp. of Parmesan cheese, grated
- 1/4 cup of butter, softened
- 2 cloves of garlic, minced
- 8 slices of ciabatta/French bread
- 2 tsp. of minced parsley (fresh) or 1/2 tsp. of parsley flakes (dried)

Directions:

- Set the air fryer up to 170°C. Spread over bread after combining the first 4 ingredients in a small dish.

- Place the bread on the tray in the air fryer basket in batches. Cook for 2 to 3 minutes or until golden brown. Serve hot.

Nutritional values per serving:

Total Calories: 122kcal, **Fats:** 7g, **Carbohydrates:** 14g, **Proteins:** 3g

Chapter 10: Air Fried Diabetic Diet - Dessert Recipes

1. Chocolate Donuts

Ready in: 18 mins.

Serves: 12

Difficulty: medium

Ingredients:

Donuts:

- ¼ cup of erythritol
- 1 cup of almond flour
- 2 tsp. of baking powder
- ½ tsp. of espresso powder
- 2 tbsp. of Cocoa Powder
- ½ tsp. of xanthan gum
- ¼ cup of melted butter
- 4 eggs (large)
- 2 tbsp. of whipping cream (heavy), 35% Cream
- ½ tsp. of vanilla extract

Chocolate Glaze:

- ½ tbsp. of butter
- ½ cup of chocolate chips, sugar-free

Directions:

- Set the air fryer to 170°C and combine dry ingredients into a large mixing bowl. Add wet ingredients and stir to thoroughly combine.
- Fill the little silicone donut moulds with the mixture after transferring them to a piping bag.
- Put the food in the air fryer basket & cook it there for 8 minutes at 170°C.
- Let the donuts cool fully before removing them from the moulds.
- Combine the butter and chocolate chips in a small bowl.
- Melt in the microwave on high for 30-second intervals. Blending between each increment.
- After the donuts have cooled, dip them in the chocolate glaze & let them dry on a rack.

Nutritional values per serving:

Total Calories: 158kcal, **Fats:** 13g, **Carbohydrates:** 3g, **Protein:** 3g

2. Peanut Butter Cookies

Ready in: 9 mins.

Serves: 8

Difficulty: easy

Ingredients:

- 1 cup of sugar substitute
- 1 beaten egg
- 1 tsp. of liquid stevia drops
- 1 cup of peanut butter, all-natural

Directions:

- Mix ingredients to make a dough.
- Create 24 balls out of the dough.
- Use a fork to push balls onto a baking sheet or cutting board to make a traditional crisscross pattern.
- Place 6-7 cookies spread out into the basket air fryer.
- Air Fry for 10 minutes at 150°C.
- After a minute or two, remove the cookies with a spatula & transfer them to a dish to complete cooling.
- Finish making the remainder of the cookies into batches.

Nutritional values per serving:

Total Calories: 198kcal, **Fats:** 17g, **Carbohydrates:** 7g, **Protein:** 9g

3. Cheesecake Bites

Ready in: 30 mins.

Serves: 5

Difficulty: medium

Ingredients:

- 1/2 cup of erythritol, plus 2 tbsp.
- 8 ounces of cream cheese
- 4 Tbsp. of heavy cream, divided
- 1/2 cup of almond flour
- 1/2 tsp. of vanilla extract

Directions:

- Give the cream cheese 20 mins to soften on the counter.
- Attach a paddle to a stand mixer.
- Blend the vanilla, softened cream cheese, heavy cream, and 1/2 cup erythritol until smooth.
- Scoop onto a baking sheet lined with parchment paper.
- Freeze until firm for about 30 minutes.
- In a small bowl, combine the 2 Tablespoons of erythritol with the almond flour.
- Roll the cheesecake bites in the mixture of almond flour after dipping them in two tablespoons of cream.
- Cook for two minutes at 145°C in an air fryer.

Nutritional values per serving:

Total Calories: 80kcal, **Fats:** 7g, **Carbohydrates:** 2g, **Protein:** 2g

4. Chocolate Cake

Ready in: 20 mins.

Serves: 6

Difficulty: medium

Ingredients:

- 1/3 cup of Truvia (0.33 g)
- 3 Eggs
- 4 tbsp. of Butter
- 1 tsp. of Vanilla extract
- 1/2 cup of Heavy Whipping Cream (119 g)
- 1/4 cup of Coconut Flour (30 g)
- 2 tbsp. of Cocoa Powder, Unsweetened
- 1 tsp. of Baking Powder
- 1/4 tsp. of Kosher Salt

For Chocolate Ganache:

- 1 tbsp. of Butter
- 3/4 cup of Heavy Whipping Cream
- 1 cup of Chocolate Chips, Sugar-Free

Directions:

- Preheat the air fryer to 170°C.
- Grease the air fryer tray and set it aside.
- Microwave the butter in a sizable mixing bowl for 30 to 60 seconds.
- Take out and add Truvia to the butter.
- Use a mixer to combine the heavy whipping cream, eggs, and vanilla extract.
- Put an end to the mixer and fill the bowl with all the dry ingredients.
- Mix again till the batter is thoroughly mixed and somewhat smooth.
- Coconut flour's absorbency varies. Mix in a bit of extra heavy whipping cream if the mixture is thicker than the typical cake batter.
- Fill the oiled tray with the batter. A toothpick inserted should come out clean after 20 minutes of air frying, and the tops should faintly bounce back when pressed.
- Let it cool.

Ganache made with chocolate:

- The chocolate chips should be put in a bowl and left alone.

- Microwave-safe bowl with heavy cream & butter heated for one minute.

- After adding the warm cream to the chocolate chips, wait a few minutes. Once the chocolate gets melted, and the mixture is smooth, stir it occasionally.

- Use the hot glaze right away, or let it cool for a bit.

- To prepare to frost, let the Ganache chill for 20 to 30 minutes before whipping the frosting with a stand mixer until it is frothy and light. This may be used as icing on top or as a filling in between layers of cake.

Nutritional values per serving:

Total Calories: 194 kcal, **Fats:** 18g, **Carbohydrates:** 5g, **Protein:** 4g

5. Cheese Biscuits
Ready in: 25 mins.

Serves: 8

Difficulty: medium

Ingredients:

- 2 tbsp. of agave nectar

- 4 tbsp. of softened butter (or some coconut oil)

- 2 tbsp. of Water

- 1 Egg

- 1/3 cup of Truvia or a half cup of sugar

- 2.5 cups of Almond Flour

- 2 tsp. of ground ginger

- ½ tsp. of Ground Nutmeg

- 1 tsp. of Ground Cinnamon

- ¼ tsp. of Kosher Salt

- 1 tsp. of Baking Soda

Directions:

- Set the Air fryer up to 170°C.

- Use parchment paper to line the cookie sheet and have it handy.

- Combine the butter, egg, agave nectar, and water in a hand blender.

- Add all of the dry ingredients to this mixture and combine thoroughly on low speed.

- Scoop out two teaspoon-sized balls, and place them on a parchment-lined baking sheet. They don't actually spread out too much, but they do leave some space between each other.

- Air fry for 12 to 15 minutes, or until the tops are just beginning to brown.

- After cooling, place the item in an airtight container. Before you consume every cookie, for instance, for the hour, they will be available.

Nutritional values per serving:

Total Calories: 122kcal, **Fats:** 10g, **Carbohydrates:** 5g, **Protein:** 3g

6. Air Fried Smores
Ready in: 7 mins.

Serves: 4

Difficulty: easy

Ingredients:

- 2 bars of chocolate

- 4 graham crackers

- 4 marshmallows

Directions:

- Use parchment paper to line the basket of the air fryer or a nonstick frying spray.

- Put graham cracker square pieces in the basket of an air fryer.

- Place a marshmallow on top of the Graham Cracker.

- Air fry the marshmallow for 7 minutes at 190°C, or until it has melted and become golden.

- Add some chocolate bar on top of the heated marshmallow and graham cracker.

- On top of a chocolate bar, place a second graham cracker.

Nutritional values per serving:

Total Calories: 165kcal, **Fats:** 7g, **Carbohydrates:** 23g, **Protein:** 2g

7. Carrot Cake
Ready in: 55 mins.

Serves: 8

Difficulty: medium

Ingredients:

- 1 tsp. of Baking Powder
- 1 ¼ cup of All Purpose Flour
- ½ tsp. of Baking Soda
- ¾ cup of Splenda
- 1 tsp. of Pumpkin Pie Spice
- 2 Eggs
- ¾ cup of Canola Oil
- 2 cups of grated Carrots, about 5 carrots (regular sized), grated

Directions:

- Set your air fryer up to 170°C and thoroughly prepare your nonstick cake pan. Mix the baking powder, flour, baking soda, and pumpkin pie spice in a mixing bowl using a fork or whisk. Next, whisk or combine the sugar substitute, eggs, and oil in a big mixing dish.

- The dry ingredients in the first bowl will be added to the big mixing bowl in the next step. Stirring in between additions, add half of the dry ingredients at a time. Next, include the carrots. After gently transferring the cake pan to a basket of air fryers, add the batter cake to the prepped cake pan.

- Check the cake's top after 30 minutes of air-frying to make sure it is not turning too black. If so, you may air fry the cake until a wooden skewer or toothpick inserted into the centre of the cake comes out clean (40 minutes total). Before

removing the cake from the pan, let it cool completely on a rack.

Nutritional values per serving:

Total Calories: 287kcal, **Fats:** 22g, Carbohydrates: 19g, **Protein:** 4g

8. Vegan Beignets
Ready in: 5 mins.

Serves: 24

Difficulty: easy

Ingredients:

For powdered baking:

- 1 tsp. of corn starch (organic)
- 1 cup of Sweetener Baking Blend

For proofing:

- 3 tbsp. of powdered baking blend
- 1 cup of coconut milk (full-fat) from a can
- 1 1/2 tsp. of active baking yeast

For dough:

- 2 tbsp. of aquafaba, can of chickpeas, drained
- 2 tbsp. of coconut oil, melted
- 3 cups of white flour (unbleached), with some extra for sprinkling on the cutting board
- 2 tsp. of vanilla

Directions:

- Fill your blender with the Baking Mix and corn starch, and blend until completely smooth.

- Heat coconut milk till it is warm yet cold enough to touch without being burned. The yeast will be killed by excessive heat. Combine it with the yeast and sugar in the bowl of a stand mixer. 10 minutes should pass for the yeast to start to froth.

- Combine the aquafaba, coconut oil, and vanilla with the yeast mixture using the paddle attachment. After that, gradually add flour to the mixture, one cup at a time.

- If you have a dough hook, switch to it after the flour has been incorporated and the dough has begun to pull away from the mixer's sides. If not, you should continue using the paddle.

- In your mixer, knead yeast dough for around 3 minutes. Even though the dough would be wetter compared to if you were baking a bread loaf, you should still be able to scoop it out and roll it into a ball without sticking it to your hands.

- Put the dough in a big bowl, cover it with a fresh dish towel, and let it rise for an hour.

- On a floured surface, roll the dough out into a rectangle which is approximately 1/3 inch thick. Before cooking, divide into 24 squares & let proof for 25-30 minutes.

- Set your air fryer's thermostat to 198°C. In your warmed air fryer basket, place paper on the bottom. You may either poke holes in the parchment or use the perforated parchment that has been trimmed to fit your basket.

- You can fit 3-6 beignets in the air fryer basket at once, based on the size of the air fryer. Just be sure to arrange them in one single layer.

- Three minutes on each side of the food. Cook for a further two minutes after flipping. You may have to cook them for an additional minute or two in your air fryer to get a golden brown colour.

- Generously top with the powdered baking mixture you created earlier and savour!

- Cook them in batches till they are all finished.

Nutritional values per serving:

Total Calories: 88kcal, **Fats:** 3g, **Carbohydrates:** 13g, **Protein:** 2g

9. Hand Pies
Ready in: 30 mins.

Serves: 8

Difficulty: medium

Ingredients:

- ¼ cup of fresh blueberries (60 mL)
- ¼ cup of blueberry jam (60 mL)
- 1 lemon
- Flour to dust
- 1 egg
- 1 package of refrigerated pie crusts, softened (14.1-oz./399-g), 2 crusts
- 2 tbsp. of sugar (30 mL)
- Oil for spritzing
- ¼ tsp. of ground cinnamon (1 mL)
- Optional: ¼ cup of powdered sugar (60 mL)

Directions:

- In a medium dish, mix the jam and blueberries. 1 teaspoon of lemon should be zested (5 mL). Add to bowl & thoroughly combine.

- The pie crust should be unrolled onto a gently dusted surface. From every piece of pie dough, cut 8 circles using a 3" (7.5 cm) biscuit cutter.

- Each circle should have 1 tiny tbsp. of filling on it. Add the rest of dough circles on top, sealing the borders with pressure. Use a fork to crimp the edges. Make 2 tiny venting vents in the centre of each pie.

- The egg is whisked in a small bowl. Apply the egg wash sparingly to the pies.

- Sprinkle the pies with the sugar-cinnamon mixture.

- Oil the cooking trays for the Air Fryer. Put 4 pies onto each baking sheet. Put a tray on the centre rack and another on the top rack.

- Set the timer for 14 minutes. Halfway through cooking, switch the cooking trays. The pies need to have a golden colour.

- Juice one teaspoon of lemon if desired. In a separate dish, whisk together the juice & powdered sugar until well combined. Drizzle all over the pies.

Nutritional values per serving:

Total Calories: 240kcal, Fats: 12g, Carbohydrates: 32g, Protein: 2g

10. Air Fried Oreos

Ready in: 10 mins.

Serves: 8

Difficulty: easy

Ingredients:

- 8 Oreo cookies
- 1 can of Crescents Dough
- 1-2 tbsp. of Powdered Sugar

Directions:

- Split apart the crescents and spread the dough over the Oreos, ensuring there aren't air bubbles and that the dough fully encases the Oreo.
- Set the air fryer to the bottom rack position and heat it at 170°C for 4 minutes before cooking the wrapped Oreos.
- After 3 to 4 minutes, or when the tops are slightly golden brown, flip the Oreos.
- Before serving, sprinkle powdered sugar over the finished Oreos.

Nutritional values per serving:

Total Calories: 159kcal, Fats: 8g, Carbohydrates: 21g, Protein: 2g

11. Apple Fritters

Ready in: 35 mins.

Serves: 10

Difficulty: medium

Ingredients:

- ½ tsp. of ground cinnamon
- ½ cup of sugar

- 1 cup of peeled & chopped apple (medium)
- 3 tbsp. of butter, melted
- 1 can of refrigerated Buttermilk Biscuits (10.2 oz.), 5 Count

Directions:

- Cooking parchment paper should be cut into two 8-inch circles. Put one round in the air fryer basket's bottom. Use cooking spray to spritz.
- Combine sugar and cinnamon in a small bowl. 2 tbsp. of the cinnamon-sugar mixture and apple, chunks should be well combined in a separate small dish.
- Divide the dough into 4-5 biscuits and then into 2 layers for each biscuit. Create a 4-inch circle out of each. Place one heaping tablespoon of the apples in the middle of each circle. Gently fold the sides over the filling and pinch them closed. 2 tbsp. of melted butter should be used to brush the biscuits all over.
- Arrange five of the biscuits in the air fryer basket on parchment paper, seam sides down. Cooking spray should be applied to the second parchment circle's top and bottom. Add a second parchment circle on top of the biscuits in the basket before adding the last five biscuits.
- Cooking time is 8 minutes at 150°C. Remove the top parchment circle, flip the biscuits with tongs, and arrange them in a single layer in the basket. Cook for another 4 to 6 minutes, or until thoroughly heated through & apples are soft. Roll remaining cinnamon-sugar mixture around biscuits before brushing with remaining 1 tbsp. Melted butter.

Nutritional values per serving:

Total Calories: 170kcal, Fats: 7g, Carbohydrates: 13g, Protein: 25g

12. Mini Double Cherry Eggrolls

Ready in: 16 mins.

Serves: 28

Difficulty: medium

Ingredients:

- ⅓ cup of cherry jam
- ½ package of cream cheese (8 ounces), softened
- ¼ cup of tart red cherries (dried), chopped
- Cooking spray (Nonstick) or 1 tbsp. of butter, melted
- 16 wonton wrappers (almost about 1/2-inch squares)
- ½ tsp. of ground cinnamon
- 3 tbsp. of sugar

Directions:

- Set the air fryer up to 205°C. Mix the cream cheese & cherry jam in a small bowl. Add the cherries, and stir. A wonton wrapper should be placed on the work surface with the corner facing you. With water, dampen the edges. Just below the middle of the wrapper, place a round spoonful of the cherry mixture.

- Bottom corner should be folded over the filling and tucked under on the opposite side. Roll the egg roll toward the last corner, folding side corners over the filling. Use the leftover wrappers and filling to repeat. Apply melted butter or nonstick frying spray to both sides of the egg rolls. In a small dish, mix the sugar with the cinnamon; leave it aside.

- Place egg rolls in the fryer basket in a single layer, if required, in batches. Cook for 4 to 5 minutes, until well browned. Take out of the air fryer. Roll immediately in cinnamon sugar using two forks. Cool onto a wire rack for five to ten minutes. Serve hot.

Nutritional values per serving:

Total Calories: 84 kcal, Fats: 3g, Carbohydrates: 14g, Protein: 1g

13. Cheesecake Chimichangas
Ready in: 20 mins.

Serves: 2

Difficulty: medium

Ingredients:

- 1/4 cup of sour cream or nonfat plain Greek yogurt
- 1 brick of cream cheese (8 ounces), softened to normal temperature
- 1½ tbsp. of granulated sugar
- 8 strawberries (medium), quartered
- 1 tsp. of pure vanilla extract
- 1 banana (medium), peeled & sliced
- 8 tsp. of Nutella
- 8 flour tortillas (soft), 8 inches
- 3 tbsp. of melted butter
- olive oil spray

Directions:

- Blend the Greek yoghurt (or sour cream), softened cream cheese, sugar, and vanilla in a mixing bowl.

- Split the mixture of cream cheese into two medium dishes and combine it with the cut bananas and strawberries in a bowl. Stir slowly to mix (or omit completely).

- A flour tortilla should be placed on a spotless work area. On the tortilla, place 1/4 of the mixture of strawberries immediately to the left of the centre. Add a spoonful of Nutella after that.

- To enclose the filling, fold the tortilla's left side over. Roll the burrito-style by tucking the short ends inside.

- Carry out the same procedure with the rest of the strawberry and banana mixtures.

- Light your air fryer to 175°C and mist the chimichangas with olive oil spray. Work in batches, arranging the chimichangas seam-side down in an equal layer, & air frying for 8-10 minutes, or till the tortilla is golden brown, based on the size of the air fryer.

- After they have been fried, put the chimichangas on a wire rack positioned over the rimmed baking sheet. Brush butter over all surfaces, including the nooks and crannies, then roll in a dish of cinnamon sugar. Repeat.

Nutritional values per serving:

Total Calories: 109 kcal, Fats: 7g, Carbohydrates: 10g, Protein: 1g

14. Strawberry Scones
Ready in: 17 mins.

Serves: 6

Difficulty: medium

Ingredients:

- 50 g of Butter
- 225 g of Self Raising Flour
- 28 g of Caster Sugar
- Egg Wash
- 60 ml of Whole Milk
- Olive Oil Spray
- Strawberries (Fresh)

Optional:

- Squirty Cream
- Strawberry Jam

Directions:

- Combine sugar and flour in a bowl. Add butter cubes.
- Mix the flour and lard together. Use your fingers to continue until the mixture resembles coarse breadcrumbs.
- Add milk until a soft dough forms. Then, on a floured surface, lay out the dough; aim for a thickness of at least 1.5 cm; any less will result in undersized scones.
- Cut your dough into medium-sized scones using cutters, and then set them in your air fryer basket.

- To avoid sticking, spray the scones' tops and sides with egg wash before placing them in the air fryer basket.
- Air fry for 4-5 minutes at 180°C, then for 2 more minutes at 160°C.
- Serve with cream, strawberry slices, and strawberry jam.

Nutritional values per serving:

Total Calories: 219kcal, Fats: 8g, Carbohydrates: 32g, Protein: 5g

15. Chocolate Soufflé
Ready in: 30 mins.

Serves: 2

Difficulty: medium

Ingredients:

- 2 tbsp. of Splenda
- 2 tbsp. of soft Butter, melted
- ¼ cup of Chocolate Chips, Sugar-Free
- 1 tbsp. of Flour
- 1.5 tbsp. of Butter
- ⅓ cup of Milk
- 2 Egg Whites & 1 Egg Yolk
- ½ tsp. of Vanilla Extract
- ½ tsp. of Cream of Tarter
- 1 tbsp. of Splenda

Directions:

- As part of the preparation, use the softened butter to "grease" each of the ramekins. After that, top them with the substitute's granulated sugar (1 tbsp. maximum for each ramekin).
- In order to distribute the sugar substitute more evenly, you may have to rotate the ramekin. Additionally, preheat the air fryer to a low level (155-165°C).
- The chocolate will then be melted. Stir after 30 seconds in a medium-sized microwave-safe basin to melt the ingredients. Alternately, and really better for chocolate, use the double boiler

technique with a basin of boiling water below. Later stages will include adding other ingredients to the bowl that this melted chocolate is in. That 1 1/2 tbsp. of butter will now be melted over low to medium heat.

- Make use of a small skillet. Whisk in the flour after the butter has melted. While whisking, wait a few minutes for the mixture to thicken. You may turn off the heat when it begins to thicken.

- During this phase, you will be multitasking. While you whisk the egg whites, we will combine the ingredients into the dish with the melted chocolate. Use a stand mixer with the whisk attachment to combine the egg whites & cream of tartar. Return to the flour & butter mixture while egg whites are being whipped to create peaks. Melted chocolate is blended with the melted butter & flour mixture. The remaining sugar substitute, vanilla essence, and egg yolks are then added. Keep an eye on the white egg mixer. When the egg whites start to form peaks, stop whisking them and carefully fold them into the mixture of other ingredients.

- Spoon the batter into the ramekins to approximately 3/4 full. The soufflés should be cooked in 12–14 minutes of air-frying.

Nutritional values per serving:

Total Calories: 288 kcal, **Fats:** 24g, **Carbohydrates:** 5g, **Protein:** 6g

16. Lemon Slice Cookies

Ready in: 5 mins.

Serves: 24

Difficulty: easy

Ingredients:

- ½ cup of Swerve granular sweetener
- ½ cup of coconut flour
- ½ tsp. of baking soda
- ½ cup of butter (unsalted), softened
- ½ tsp. of salt

- 1 tbsp. of lemon juice
- ½ tsp. of liquid vanilla stevia
- ¼ tsp. of lemon extract, optional
- Icing
- 2 egg yolks
- ⅔ cup of Swerve confectioners sweetener
- 3 tsp. of lemon juice

Directions:

- Swerve, salt, baking soda, and coconut flour should all be mixed in a stand mixer.

- Mix the dry ingredients well after adding the melted butter, including all ingredients, excluding the egg yolks. If necessary, add alternative sweetener and/or lemon essence after tasting the batter to adjust the sweetness and lemon taste to your liking. After that, stir in the yolks until well combined.

- The batter should be put in the middle of a big piece of plastic wrap that has been placed on the counter. Form a log with the wrap by rolling it over the dough & cutting off the excess. For 2 to 3 hours or overnight, refrigerate after firmly wrapping.

- Set the air fryer's thermostat to 155°C. The air fryer's basket should be greased. Unwrap the log, then slice half of it into cookies that are 14 inches thick. Put the leftover batter in the refrigerator. In the basket of air fryers, arrange as many cookie slices as you can into a single layer. Cook the cookies for approximately 3 to 5 minutes, or till the edges are golden. Before removing the basket to totally cool on a wire rack, give it time to cool inside the basket for two minutes. Use the leftover dough to repeat. After cooling, add frosting.

- Set the oven up to 170°C. Cut the log of cookies into 14-inch-thick pieces after unwrapping. A baking sheet pan with parchment paper should have cookies on it spaced about one inch apart. The edges should brown after 8 to 10 minutes of baking. Let cool for two to three minutes before transferring to the wire rack to finish cooling before frosting.

- In a small bowl, combine the confectioners and lemon juice. On top of the cooled cookies, drizzle.

Nutritional values per serving:

Total Calories: 66 kcal, Fats: 6g, Carbohydrates: 2g, Protein: 1g

17. Air Fried Brownie
Ready in: 6 mins.

Serves: 2

Difficulty: easy

Ingredients:

- 3 tbsp. of almond flour
- 1 tbsp. of butter, melted
- 1 1/2 tbsp. of monk fruit sweetener
- 1/2 tsp. of baking powder
- 1 tbsp. of cocoa powder
- , a pinch of salt
- 2 tbsp. of chocolate chips, sugar-free
- 1 egg white

Directions:

- In a small ramekin, melt the butter and stir in the sweetener, almond flour, baking soda, salt, cocoa powder, and egg white. Keep in mind that the mixture would be thick and to only stir until everything is mixed. It will be shiny, much like a brownie mix from a box. Add the chocolate chunks and stir.

- For 3 minutes, preheat your air fryer up to 155°C. Add the ramekin into the air fryer that has been warmed.

- Give 6-minute cook time: This will probably result in fudgy brownies which are fully cooked on the outside but somewhat underdone in the middle.

- 8 minutes of cooking time will probably result in brownies that are fully cooked.

- Wait one minute before eating the brownie.

Nutritional values per serving:

Total Calories: 254 kcal, Fats: 16g, Carbohydrates: 7.6g, Protein: 7.7g

18. Chocolate Air Fried Molten Lava Cakes
Ready in: 20 mins.

Serves: 4

Difficulty: medium

Ingredients:

- 1/2 cup of butter (unsalted), cubed. / cooking spray (non-stick).

- 4 oz. of good quality chocolate (unsweetened), finely chopped

- 2 eggs

- 1/4 cup of All-Purpose Pure Organic Stevia Blend

- 2 egg yolks

- Pinch of salt

- 1/2 cup of whipping cream (35%)

- 2 tbsp. of flour

Directions:

- Set your air fryer's temperature to 185°C.

- Spray or lightly grease four 4-ounce oven-safe ramekins, then put aside.

- Set up a double boiler by placing a heat-resistant bowl over boiling water. Stir the butter and chocolate into the hot water to melt them.

- In a bowl, egg yolks, whisk eggs, flour, & Pure Organic Stevia blend using an electric mixer set to medium-high speed.

- Add one pinch of salt & keep whisking until the mixture becomes thick and pale.

- Once the mixture has thickened, reduce the speed of the mixer to low & gently add the chocolate till well incorporated.

- After that, evenly pour the chocolate mixture into the ramekins that have been prepared.

- Air-fried the lava cakes for 8-10 minutes, or until they are puffy and have a thin crust around the sides.

- Check on and gently remove the ramekins using silicone oven mitts or a kitchen towel. The cakes must jiggle and be mushy in the middle for the "lava" to flow. If required, extend the time.

- Use a knife to smooth the edges of the ramekin cakes before serving the molten lava cakes. Turn the cakes over onto the serving platter and top each with a dab of whipped cream.

- Whipping cream may be used to make homemade whipped cream by beating it in a bowl till soft peaks form whilst the cakes are cooling.

- The Pure Organic Stevia Blend should then be added.

- Whip for a further minute.

Nutritional values per serving:

Total Calories: 530 kcal, **Fats:** 54g, Carbohydrates: 26g, **Protein:** 9g

19. Chocolate Muffins
Ready in: 14 mins.

Serves: 6

Difficulty: medium

Ingredients:

- 60 g of Milk Chocolate
- 10 Squares of Chocolate
- 30 g of Self Raising Flour
- 1 Tsp. of Butter heaped
- 15 g of Cocoa Powder
- 1 Tsp. of Honey
- 1 Tsp. of Vanilla Essence optional
- 1 Tsp. of Single Cream

Directions:

- Combine chocolate pieces, butter, and honey in the air fryer baking dish. Melt the chocolate by placing it into the air

fryer & cooking it for two minutes at 120°C.

- Add single cream and stir. Now it will be smooth and gorgeous. After that, add the crushed chocolate to the dish containing the flour & cocoa powder together with the melted chocolate.

- If using vanilla, add it now. Give it a Good stirring Load into the air fryer muffin cases.

- Give it 10 minutes to cook at 160 °C.

Nutritional values per serving:

Total Calories: 97kcal, **Fats:** 6g, **Carbohydrates:** 13g, **Protein:** 2g

20. Pound Cake
Ready in: 30 mins.

Serves: 8

Difficulty: easy

Ingredients:

- ½ tsp. of Baking Powder
- 1 ¾ cup of Flour
- ½ cup of softened Butter at normal temperature
- ½ tsp. of Vanilla Extract
- ½ lb. of Splenda, 1 cup plus 2 tbsp.

Directions:

- Set your air fryer up to 170°C. Prepare the cake pan by using at least two of the following techniques: greasing, flouring, or using parchment paper that has already been cut to size.

- Combine the flour and baking powder in a mixing dish using a whisk or sifter.

- Next, combine the butter and sugar substitute in a new mixing dish.

- Add each egg 1 at a time, carefully swirling in between. The vanilla extract is then added.

- The mixture of flour from the first bowl will be added to the mixing bowl in the next step. Stir just enough to mix. Add a teaspoon, or more if necessary, of whipping cream or another dairy product if it looks too thick.

- Pour the prepared cake pan with the batter until it is approximately 1/2 to 2/3 filled. Based on size of your pan, you could have batter remaining. Place the pan into the air fryer. A toothpick inserted in the middle of the cake should come out clean after 15 to 20 minutes of baking. Based on size of the air fryer, baking times may vary. Take care while removing the pan of cake since it probably will be hot.

- Let the cake cool completely before taking it out of the pan.

Nutritional values per serving:

Total Calories: 234 kcal, Fats: 14g, Carbohydrates: 21g, Protein: 6g

21. Cinnamon Bread Twists

Ready in: 30 mins.

Serves: 6

Difficulty: easy

Ingredients:

For Bread Twists Dough:

- 1 tsp. of Baking Powder

- 1 cup of All Purpose Flour (120g)

- 2/3 cup of Greek Yogurt, Fat-Free (150g)

- 1/4 tsp. of Kosher Salt

For Brushing:

- 2 Tbsp. of Granulated Sugar (24g)

- 2 Tbsp. of Light Butter (28g)

- 1-2 tsp. of Ground Cinnamon

Directions:

- Before mixing the Greek yoghurt, combine the baking powder, flour, and salt. Everything should be combined with a fork till a crumbly dough forms. There should be some dry flour left in the bowl.

- Place the dough on a flat surface & shape it into a single, round ball. The dough should be divided into six 45-gram portions. The dough pieces should be rolled into thin, 8" long strips between your hands or on a flat surface.

- Form a shape of a ribbon by folding the end of every strip over, then place the ribbon on an oiled air fryer basket. Spray the top of the basket with cooking spray after placing all 6 bread twists within, then shut the lid.

- Air fry for 15 minutes at 170°C. (Or just bake for 25–30 minutes onto a baking sheet @ 190°C)

- Near the finish of cooking, melt the butter in the microwave, then stir in the sugar and cinnamon. When the bread twists are taken out of the air fryer, immediately brush them with the cinnamon sugar butter. Serve hot.

Nutritional values per serving:

Total Calories: 120kcal, Fats: 12g, Carbohydrates: 2g, Protein: 2g

22. Apple Chips

Ready in: 35 mins.

Serves: 10

Difficulty: easy

Ingredients:

- 3/4 tsp. of ground cinnamon

- large crisp, sweet apples

- a pinch salt

Directions:

- Start by giving your apples a good cleaning.

- When chopping apples, you have the option of leaving the seeds in or coring them. It works both ways. Use a mandolin or a sharp knife to produce rounds that are approximately 1/8 of one inch thick after they have been cleaned and cored.

- Set the air fryer up to 198°C. Combine salt and cinnamon in a medium bowl if you're using both. If not, sprinkle the apple slices with cinnamon and place them in a layer at the base of the basket. Just enough slices must be placed to create one single layer without any overlap.

- Cook the slices of apple for 8 minutes, turning them over halfway through. You may take the crisped apples out of the fryer if you find them to be just right, then cook the remaining apples as necessary.

- Increase the air fryer's cooking time a little if you need the food to be crispier. Only add 1 minute at one time till the appropriate crisp level is obtained, according to our advice.

Nutritional values per serving:

Total Calories: 65kcal, **Fats:** 0g, **Carbohydrates:** 18g, **Protein:** 0g

23. Cinnamon Apple Empanadas
Ready in: 25 mins.

Serves: 12

Difficulty: medium

Ingredients:

- 2 apples, any
- 12 thawed empanada wrappers
- 2 tbsp. of raw honey
- 1 tsp. of cinnamon
- 1 tsp. of vanilla extract
- 1/8 tsp. of nutmeg
- 1 tsp. of water
- 2 tsp. of cornstarch
- Cooking oil.
- 1 egg, beaten

Directions:

- Set a saucepan over a medium-high flame. Apples, nutmeg, cinnamon, honey, & vanilla should all be added. The apples should be tender after 2–3 minutes of stirring and cooking.

- In a small bowl, combine the water and cornstarch. Stir after adding to the pan. For 30 seconds, cook.

- Before adding the filling to the empanada wrappers, let the mixture cool for at least five minutes.

- The empanada wrappers should be placed on a level surface. In water, dunk a frying brush. Make sure the edges of each empanada wrapper are sealed with a wet brush. The crust will get softer, as a result, making rolling simpler.

- Fill each with the apple mixture. For each empanada, add 1 spoonful of the apple mixture. Never overfill. Use a spoon to spread the mixture out.

- Tuck the empanadas in. Create indentations in the crust with a fork to enclose the empanadas around the edges. Along each edge, pierce the crust with the fork.

- Spray cooking oil on the air fryer basket. Empanadas should be added to the basket of the Air Fryer. Avoid piling the empanadas. If necessary, cook in batches.

- Apply the beaten egg to the top of every empanada using a frying brush (egg wash).

- The Air Fryer should be set at 205°C. Cook until crisp, about 8 to 10 minutes.

- Before serving, cool.

Nutritional values per serving:

Total Calories: 164kcal, **Fats:** 1g, **Carbohydrates:** 0g, **Protein:** 5g

24. Air Fried Banana
Ready in: 10 mins.

Serves: 2

Difficulty: easy

Ingredients:

- 1/4 tsp. of cinnamon
- 1 banana (ripe), cut in half-inch slices
- 1/2 tsp. of brown sugar
- 1 tbsp. of Chopped nuts (toasted) to taste
- 1 tbsp. of Granola

Directions:

- Combine the brown sugar and cinnamon in a small bowl; leave aside.

- Grease a small baking pan sparingly. Slice the bananas and add them to the pan. The banana should be sprayed with oil before being dusted with cinnamon sugar. For about 4-5 minutes, air fried at 200°C.

- When serving, top the banana with some granola and almonds.

Nutritional values per serving:

Total Calories: 113kcal, **Fats:** 4g, **Carbohydrates:** 19g, **Protein:** 2g

25. Strawberry Turnovers
Ready in: 40 mins.

Serves: 12

Difficulty: easy

Ingredients:

- ¾ cup of finely chopped strawberries
- 1 pie crust (store-bought or homemade)
- 2 tbsp. of sugar
- half lemon zest
- ½ tsp. of vanilla
- 1 tbsp. of cornstarch
- Sugar for sprinkling
- 1 beaten egg

Directions:

- On a floured board, roll out pie dough to a thickness of approximately 1/4". Cut as many dough circles out as you can using the round cookie cutter. Take the leftovers and create a new ball if necessary. Once again, roll out your dough and cut out additional rounds to make a total of 12 pieces.

- In a mixing dish, combine the diced strawberries with vanilla, sugar, lemon zest, & cornstarch. On each round, spoon 1 to 2 Tbsp. of filling.

- Apply egg wash to the circular edges & fold in half. To seal the edges, use a fork. Make 3 slits on the top of turnovers with a sharp knife. The turnovers' tops are brushed with egg wash and dusted with sugar.

- For a short while, preheat your air fryer to 170°C. Spray nonstick cooking spray on the air fryer basket. Make sure there is space between each turnover for hot air to flow. Put 5–6 turnovers in the air fryer basket and cook for 10 minutes, or till the crust is brownish golden. The pastries may be taken out with tongs and put onto a wire rack or dish to cool. Continue with the remaining pies.

Nutritional values per serving:

Total Calories: 91kcal, **Fats:** 4.7g, **Carbohydrates:** 10.7g, **Proteins:** 1.2g

Chapter 11: Healthy 28-Days Meal Plan

A healthy 28-day meal plan is given below, including all the recipes already mentioned in the previous chapters of this book. According to the recipes present in this book, an everyday meal plan is divided into 3 meals a day.

Week 1:

Day 1:

Daytime:

- Italian-Style Beef Meatballs
- Coconut Shrimp

Evening:

- Coconut Crusted Air Fried Turkey Fingers

Night time:

- Air Fried Meatloaf
- Fried Spicy Green Beans

Day 2:

Daytime:

- Lamb Meatball Kebabs
- Sweet Potato Nachos

Evening:

- Turkey Croquettes

Night time:

- Bacon Hot Dogs
- Rosemary-Garlic Brussels Sprouts

Day 3:

Daytime:

- Steak Bites
- Red Potatoes

Evening:

- Fish & Chips

Night time:

- Juicy Pork Chops
- Delicious Radishes

Day 4:

Daytime:

- Air fried Brats
- Breaded Summer Squash

Evening:

- Crusted Sweet Potato Chicken Nuggets

Night time:

- Thai Air Fried Chicken Meatballs
- Herb & Lemon Cauliflower

Day 5:

Daytime:

- Chicken Cutlets
- Air-Fried Asparagus

Evening:

- Potato Chips

Night time:

- Leg of Lamb
- Green Tomato Stacks

Day 6:

Daytime:

- Lobster Tails with Garlic-Lemon Butter
- Air-Fried Roasted Green Beans

Evening:

- Cauliflower Gnocchi & Marinara Sauce

Night time:

- Spicy Bay Scallops

Day 7:

Daytime:

- Lamb & Cauliflower Rice
- Crispy bacon

Evening:

- Bacon Wrapped Scallops

Night time:

- Crumbed Fish
- Air Fried Vegetables

Week 2:

Day 1:

Daytime:

- Meat Filled Air Fried Pita Pockets
- Crispy Garlic Croutons

Evening:

- Feta Beets

Night time:

- Lamb Spicy Curry Puffs
- Air Fried Cabbage

Day 2:

Daytime:

- Stuffed Turkey Peppers
- Jalapeño Bacon Wrapped Poppers

Evening:

- Cinnamon Apples

Night time:

- Chicken Cordon Bleu
- Air-Fried Okra

Day 3:

Daytime:

- Nashville Delicious Hot Chicken
- Crispy Chickpeas

Evening:

- Zucchini Fries

Night time:

- Mustard Honey Turkey Breast
- Air-Fried Zucchini

Day 4:

Daytime:

- Air Fried Lamb & Potatoes
- Air-Fried Plantains

Evening:

- Chicken Wings

Night time:

- Lemon Pepper Shrimp
- Air-Fried Carrots

Day 5:

Daytime:

- Crispy Parmesan Cod
- Air-Fried Eggplant

Evening:

- Bolognese Zucchini Boats

Night time:

- Paneer Tikka Fry
- Blooming Onions

Day 6:

Daytime:

- Zucchini Pizza
- Air-Fried Broccoli

Evening:

- Onion Rings

Night time:

- Stuffed Okra
- Air-Fried Spaghetti Squash

Day 7:

Daytime:

- Braised Delicious Lamb-shanks
- Crispy Chickpea

Evening:

- Crab Rangoon

Night time:

- Jamaican Chicken Curry
- Jalapeño Bacon Wrapped Poppers

Week 3:

Day 1:

Daytime:

- Piccata Chicken Pockets
- Blooming Onions

Evening:

- Air Fried Churros

Night time:

- Pork Skewers with Sauce
- Air Fried Cabbage

Day 2:

Daytime:

- Zucchini Filled With Hamburger
- Air-Fried Okra

Evening:

- Egg Rolls

Night time:

- Frozen Pork Meatballs
- Green Tomato Stacks

Day 3:

Daytime:

- Feta Lemon Chicken
- Crispy Garlic Croutons

Evening:

- Stuffed Mushrooms

Night time:

- Healthy Chicken & Veggies
- Air-Fried Plantains

Day 4:

Daytime:

- Mushroom Egg Turkey Burgers
- Air-Fried Asparagus

Evening:

- Pretzel Bites

Night time:

- Rotisserie Chicken
- Herb & Lemon Cauliflower

Day 5:

Daytime:

- Spaghetti & Lamb meatball muffins

- Air-Fried Roasted Green Beans

Evening:

- Pretzel Dogs

Night time:

- Lamb kebab
- Crispy Bacon

Day 6:

Daytime:

- Stuffed Lamb Feta Burgers
- Breaded Summer Squash

Evening:

- Air-Fried Ravioli

Night time:

- Salmon Nuggets
- Delicious Radishes

Day 7:

Daytime:

- Chili Lime Tilapia
- Jalapeño Bacon Wrapped Poppers

Evening:

- Cheeseburger Onion Rings

Night time:

- Swordfish Steak & Mango Citrus Salsa
- Air-Fried Okra

Week 4:

Day 1:

Daytime:

- Air Fried Tofu
- Fried Spicy Green Beans

Evening:

- Sriracha Crispy Spring Rolls

Night time:

- Onion Bites
- Sweet Potato Nachos

Day 2:

Daytime:

- Tandoori Cauliflower
- Crispy Garlic Croutons

Evening:

- Air-Fried Calamari

Night time:

- Beetroot Cutlet
- Air-Fried Plantains

Day 3:

Daytime:

- Crispy Corn Fritters
- Crispy Bacon

Evening:

- Mushroom Roll-Ups

Night time:

- Cajun Potatoes
- Herb & Lemon Cauliflower

Day 4:

Daytime:

- Eggplant Parmesan Pasta
- Air Fried Asparagus

Evening:

- Garlic Bread

Night time:

- Kale & Sweet Potato Calzones
- Air-Fried Zucchini

Day 5:

Daytime:

- Stuffed Bitter Gourd
- Air Fried Carrots

Evening:

- Chocolate Donuts

Night time:

- Pumpkin Pie

- Coconut Shrimp

Day 6:

Daytime:

- Italian-Style Beef Meatballs
- Coconut Shrimp

Evening:

- Coconut Crusted Air Fried Turkey Fingers

Night time:

- Air Fried Meatloaf
- Fried Spicy Green Beans

Day 7:

Daytime:

- Lamb Meatball Kebabs
- Sweet Potato Nachos

Evening:

- Turkey Croquettes

Night time:

- Bacon Hot Dogs
- Rosemary-Garlic Brussels Sprouts

Cooking Measurement Chart

COOKING CONVERSION CHART

Measurement

CUP	ONCES	MILLILITERS	TABLESPOONS
8 cup	64 oz	1895 ml	128
6 cup	48 oz	1420 ml	96
5 cup	40 oz	1180 ml	80
4 cup	32 oz	960 ml	64
2 cup	16 oz	480 ml	32
1 cup	8 oz	240 ml	16
3/4 cup	6 oz	177 ml	12
2/3 cup	5 oz	158 ml	11
1/2 cup	4 oz	118 ml	8
3/8 cup	3 oz	90 ml	6
1/3 cup	2.5 oz	79 ml	5.5
1/4 cup	2 oz	59 ml	4
1/8 cup	1 oz	30 ml	3
1/16 cup	1/2 oz	15 ml	1

Temperature

FAHRENHEIT	CELSIUS
100 °F	37 °C
150 °F	65 °C
200 °F	93 °C
250 °F	121 °C
300 °F	150 °C
325 °F	160 °C
350 °F	180 °C
375 °F	190 °C
400 °F	200 °C
425 °F	220 °C
450 °F	230 °C
500 °F	260 °C
525 °F	274 °C
550 °F	288 °C

Weight

IMPERIAL	METRIC
1/2 oz	15 g
1 oz	29 g
2 oz	57 g
3 oz	85 g
4 oz	113 g
5 oz	141 g
6 oz	170 g
8 oz	227 g
10 oz	283 g
12 oz	340 g
13 oz	369 g
14 oz	397 g
15 oz	425 g
1 lb	453 g

Conclusion

Your body can't effectively handle and use the glucose from your diet if you have diabetes. There are several forms of diabetes, each form with its own origins, but they are all characterised by an excess of glucose in the blood. Insulin and/or medicines are used as treatments. Adopting a healthier diet may help avoid certain kinds of diabetes. You have a lot of options for preventing the onset of diabetes. But if you start to have diabetic symptoms, visit a doctor. Diabetes may be treated and controlled more effectively the earlier it is identified and treated. Your chances of living a long, healthy life increase with how well you can regulate your blood sugar level.

It's crucial to consume the correct quantity of meals each day if you have diabetes. In order to receive the proper quantity of carbohydrates in every meal or snack, the eating plan will contain information on how much to consume. You'll have to discover how to weigh your meals and count carbohydrates. It's also critical to eat at the appropriate times. To prevent having low or high blood sugar levels, you should make plans for frequent, balanced meals. It might be beneficial to have about the same quantity of carbohydrates at each meal. Your eating plan would also show you how to follow it both at home and in restaurants.

Without a doubt, a diabetic person can utilize the air fryer often to prepare healthful meals. The food you choose to cook in an appliance will have a greater impact on its suitability than the equipment itself. You have a fantastic opportunity with the air fryer to prepare healthier cuisine with fewer calories, less acrylamide generation, few Tran's fats, and better nutrient retention. Having said that, the air fryer doesn't miraculously turn harmful meals into healthful treats for our bodies. It's crucial to do an analysis of the food to learn what it contains since the decisions you make could still have an impact on you.

Made in the USA
Middletown, DE
25 September 2023

39365280R00073